GRIEF

A Dark, Sacred Time

Darrelyn Gunzburg

Flying Horse Books

Published in 2019 by
Flying Horse Books
an imprint of The Wessex Astrologer Ltd
PO Box 9307
Swanage
BH19 9BF

For a full list of our titles go to www.wessexastrologer.com

Cover design by Jonathan Taylor

Cover photograph by David Krasnostein
www.flaneurimages.com

A catalogue record for this book is available at The British Library

ISBN 9781910531341

CONTENTS

Other books by Darrelyn Gunzburg

Life After Grief
An Astrological Guide to Dealing with Loss
(The Wessex Astrologer 2004)

AstroGraphology
*The Hidden Link Between Your Horoscope and Your
Handwriting*
(The Wessex Astrologer 2009)

As Editor

The Imagined Sky: Cultural Perspectives.
(Equinox Publishing, 2016)

Space, Place and Religious Landscapes: Living Mountains
(with Bernadette Brady)
(Bloomsbury Academic, forthcoming)

Published Plays

Hiccup
(Currency Press Ltd, 1989)

Behind the Beat
(Currency Press Ltd, 1990)

'Water from the Well', in *Around the Edge: Women's Plays.
(*edited by Diane Brown. Adelaide: Tantrum Press, 1990)

'A Touchy Subject' *(with Margaret Fischer and Roxxy Bent)*
in *Weighing It up & a Touchy Subject.*
(Adelaide: Tantrum Press, 1989)

For Bernadette

Acknowledgements

Thank you Grandpa Isaac Gunzburg. It took many years for me to recognise that you were my gatekeeper to childhood loss and how, in working with the clay of my grief for you, I entered a world that contained great treasures.

Thank you Mal McKissock. Your inspirational workshops through NALAG (National Association for Loss and Grief) in Sydney, Australia set me sailing on my voyage to the land of conscious grief in 1982.

Thank you John W. James and Russell Friedman. Your work extended my knowledge and allowed me to find a pathway through unresolved grief.

Thank you to all of my courageous and willing students, clients, friends, and people who attended my lectures and allowed me to nudge and tap at the well of your grief. While you were all happy to let me publish your stories, I have respected your wishes to remain anonymous, in particular Ewan, whose reaction when he heard I was writing this book was: 'I'd like a book about grief that, when you open it up, just says: "My God, that's dreadful, how on earth can you cope?" and then listens to you cry for four hours.'

Thank you Michael Clancy for permission to use your photograph on p.161.

Thank you David Krasnostein for your creativity, generosity, and skill with the cover photograph.

Thank you Margaret Cahill. You first heard me lecture on this subject in Reading, England, in September 2000, saw its potential as a book and was patient enough to midwife its first expression as *Life After Grief* in 2004. Revisiting the material with you for a different audience fifteen years on has been a painful joy. We cried anew at those who struggled to give voice to their grief and wept with joy as those stories emerged. However often I revisit these stories, there is astonishment at how well we heal. More than this, for me re-engaging with these journeys of loss has been an encounter with a previous self, retracing those paths with mature eyes, seeing anew the dilemmas and confusions that grief brings and recognising that grief is still Secret Mourning Business, only understood by those who have encountered it. For enabling people to encounter it through this book as a way of offering resources before they need it, for your diligence, support, enthusiasm for life, and being editorially brilliant, my love and respect for you as a publisher and a friend remains unbounded.

Thank you Bernadette. I owe you more than it is possible to note for the love, wisdom, and perception that you shine on all that I do.

Introduction

This book is about letting go. Specifically, it is about letting go of life as you knew it when death comes to call. It is about letting go of the master plan so carefully mapped out about length of life and the attainment of things worthwhile and which segues to another gig where the musicians are unknown and the music riffs in a language you have never heard before. This book is also about walking forwards into your future when that future seems over, a space without time, a time without end, when there is no fire in the grate and the pilot light is out. It takes courage to walk that journey across the sullen earth to sorrow's end. If you are someone who is huddling in the rain and darkness of inconsolable loss, wondering how you will ever have the strength once more to put one step ahead of the other, know that across the sweep and tract of grief there is a lodestar in encountering loss. The lodestar is to recognise that grief is a journey, not an event, and that it opens a door to a different part of your life.

The experience of grief is among the most fundamental and inescapable aspects of the human and animal condition. Western society acknowledges it as a profound truth in literature, film, theatre, art and music, for the poet, the writer, and the artist are the touchstones of society who express this heightened awareness of intense emotion for the rest of society. Who could fail to be affected by writer Isabel Allende's heart-rending lament for her daughter Paula?[1] Who could remain untouched by Julie's pain when a fatal car crash kills her husband and young daughter in *Blue*, Part One of Krzysztof Kieslowski's *Three Colours* trilogy? Although gay marriage is law in many countries now, it wasn't back in 1994 when Richard Curtis wrote the screenplay for *Four Weddings and A Funeral*. The funeral was that of Gareth, the large, flamboyant homosexual who wore colourful and extravagant waistcoats. Screenwriter Richard Curtis has Gareth's lover, Matthew, open the eulogy in this way:

> Gareth used to prefer funerals to weddings. He said
> it was easier to get enthusiastic about a ceremony one
> at least had an outside chance of eventually being
> involved in.'[2]

Artists are the seers of society. They allow us to feel by proxy. They encourage us to encounter the intensity of loss through death by the situations they construct in ink, pigment, light, music, shape, and form, flagging this most intense of experiences as one we, too, will have to face in our unique way, for human emotion has not changed in quality throughout recorded history. Poets, writers, dancers, artists and musicians have never allowed death to become a taboo subject. Why has it become so for the rest of us?

This work emerged slowly, initially from attending several workshops with Mal McKissock, in Sydney, Australia, which gave me an insight into the process of grief. This understanding accompanied me into my studies at NIDA and resulted in me writing my final thesis for my Diploma in Directing on grief in theatre, followed by several produced and published plays dealing with loss. I encountered the work of John W. James and Russell Friedman and quietly worked through the book with a friend, each allowing the other the space to grieve unfinished losses.[3] Between March 2000 and April 2003, I conducted qualitative research talking with people about their grief in semi-structured interviews of an hour and a half in length using a questionnaire based on that in *The Grief Recovery Handbook*. Those findings formed the essence of this book. While people grieve many things, the principal aim of this book is to look at grief specifically as it relates to death and to present ways to effectively help you if you are grieving from the death of someone close to you.

North Devon, England
February 2019

Notes

1.   Isabel Allende. *Paula*. Barcelona: Plaza & Jane, 1994.
2.   Richard Curtis, *Four Weddings and a Funeral (Screenplay)* (London: Working Title Films, 1993).pp.94-96.
3.   John W. James, and Russell Friedman. *The Grief Recovery Handbook*. New York: Harper Collins, 1998.

The Myth of Grief:
Lying Down with the Seals

Death is the uninvited guest in our lives, the unexpected visitor, and it has to be that way otherwise we couldn't live fully and functionally. Death walks towards us, however, carrying Grief in her arms and Grief has to be honoured immediately Death arrives. The difficulty is that we are not taught how to do this. Most bodies of knowledge in the West deny the grief we will all have to encounter at some stage in our lives, seeing it as a one-off event. Yet there is a myth of grief which has been quite neglected, and it is the myth of Proteus, the son of Tethys and Oceanus, and Menelaus, the husband of Helen, who fought for ten long years in the Trojan War.

We are told in Homer's *The Odyssey* (IV.351-481) that, after the war, Menelaus and his men wandered a further eight years in the Mediterranean. Finally, on the verge of returning home, their ships were kept idle for twenty days on the isle of Pharos on the Egyptian coast,

> in the rolling seas off the mouth of the Nile, a day's sail
> out for a well-found vessel with a roaring wind astern.[1]

Now this island was the home of the immortal seer Proteus, the Old Man of the Sea who owed allegiance to Poseidon and kept guard over Poseidon's herd of seals. Each day at noon he emerged from the waves and counted the herd, and then moved to the shelter of a cave and lay down amongst them, 'those children of the brine, the flippered seals.' It was Proteus' daughter, Eidothee, who took pity on the starving Menelaus and gave him the solution. 'Disguise yourself in sealskin,' she told him, 'and wait for my father to lie down with the seals. Then grasp his hands and ask him why this has happened and how you can make amends. But,' she warned, 'my father never speaks oracularly unless forced to do so and he can change shape at will. Do not be intimidated by these changes. Hold onto him tightly and when he realises you will not be shaken, then he will admit defeat and answer your questions faithfully.'

Becalmed by the weather and unable to proceed home, Menelaus had little choice. He covered himself in sealskins and gently lay down with the seals; and as Eidothee had said it would happen, so it happened. At noon, Proteus emerged from the waves and one by one he counted the herd. Satisfied he moved to the shelter of the cave and with the protective gesture of a loving shepherd and the sigh of a job well done, he lowered his aged body and he, too, lay down amongst his seals.

Immediately Menelaus sprang up and seized Proteus with both hands. Proteus gave a shout of alarm. Instantly he changed into a bearded lion whose roar echoed across the recesses of the land. His rapier-sharp teeth slashed without warning and Menelaus trembled in his shoes, but he remembered Eidothee's words and he held on tight. The lion cavorted, desperate to shake him off, but Menelaus hung on. Then a mighty dragon stood in his place, his scales glinting in the sun, breathing fire as hot as a furnace. Menelaus' body shrieked from the heat, but he remembered Eidothee's words and he tightened his grip. The dragon paced and bellowed, smoke rose and choked Menelaus, yet still he did not loosen his hold. Then the dragon disappeared and a powerful panther paced the forest floor. Menelaus' skin grazed and shredded as the panther ran through the undergrowth, but he remembered Eidothee's words and he held on tenaciously. Then he found himself gripping the tough hide of a giant boar whose long tusks thrust menacingly at Menelaus. He could smell the fear in his own sweat, but he heard Eidothee's words, 'Stay with the process, don't be intimated by the changes.' Then the boar was gone and he was drifting out to sea, carried deep, deep to the ocean floor… Just as he was thinking, 'Now, now I can let go,' he came to with a jolt! He hadn't let go his grip, but he had come perilously close to doing so. He struggled to the surface, knuckles still clenched, lungs bursting and greedily gasped in lungfuls of salt air, kicking valiantly to stay above the slapping waves. Then the sea disappeared and his legs were no longer pushing against the weight of the ocean, but against the trunk of a great tree in leaf. The cover of leaves reached far above him and cool air licked at his face. The invigorating smell of forest air was intoxicating. He felt life surge back through his body, rejuvenated and as strong as this great tree whose roots reached far into the earth for sustenance, and whose canopy embraced the sky. And a voice said to him: 'Who are you who has maintained your grip on me, despite where I have taken you? Who are you who has endured suffering and misery, desolation and despair that you may see my true face?' Then Menelaus looked around him and he saw an old man whose eyes told of a pained and wounded life and whose aged face was writ with the lines of anguish and torment, and he realised he was looking into the face of Life itself and that behind the pain there was the light of understanding and wisdom, love and courage. Gently

Proteus released Menelaus' grip from his shoulders and he massaged the hands that had refused to give in.

And Menelaus spoke, saying, 'Show me the way home. Tell me what I must do to start the winds playing amidst the sails of my ship,' and Proteus answered, 'You omitted to make due sacrifice to Zeus before the journey began. Now you must revisit the heaven-fed waters of the Nile and make ceremonial offerings to the gods who live in the broad sky. When that is done, the gods will grant you the journey you desire.' Menelaus did as Proteus said and he returned home, home to his mundane life in Sparta with Helen and a changed world; and the cycle and process of grief was completed.

* * *

Myths are not simply stories told to please children. They were the way that ancient cultures made sense of the world. They contained inherent behaviour patterns that explained the human mindset and made it possible to choose responses that were ethically and morally viable. They answered the basic questions: Who am I? Where have I come from? Where am I going? How do I live during the journey? Myths externalised the psychology of the ancient world, for divinity was seen in everything and it was thought that all life contained answers. Today, myths continue to illustrate human qualities and behavioural attitudes that remain unchanging over time, inviting us to understand them, develop the themes offered and rise above the plot to reinterpret or even change the endings through our own wisdom. While most myths describe an unfolding journey, however, the myth of grief is made of a totally different texture, for grief always enters our lives without notice and so this myth only comes alive once the person's context and history has empowered it: '... and Proteus turned into ... (you add your ferocious animal in here).' What is it that you fear? What is it that you have been taught about loss and letting go that makes this such a dreaded process?

In Menelaus' encounter with Proteus, Homer illustrated the process of grief. Like Menelaus, we think we are on a journey, but grief comes unexpectedly and keeps us idle in a sheltered cove, laid off-course and uncertain of how to proceed. The island is the home of the immortal seer Proteus, who can only use his gift of prophecy to answer questions about the future if he is captured. Proteus' daughter, Eidothee, gives Menelaus the solution, suggesting he hide himself amongst the seals until Proteus is asleep. One can interpret seals as representing our instincts. We are, however, so often socialised not to talk about our grief that we can't hear that inner voice and the grief becomes stuck. We call this repressed or unresolved grief, articulated through Menelaus being caught in the bay, unable to move forward. Only by going inward into the process of grief to face this dramatically changeable, emotional energy that floods, erupts, and shatters our mundane lives can we gain any answers. These answers, however, don't come directly: we have to stay with the process through all its varying disguises - pain, bodily distress, panic, sadness, isolation, and confusion. Finally Proteus turns into a great tree in leaf, telling us that at the end of the process we emerge stronger for the journey and embracing the Tree of Life from which new growth can occur. The last leg of the journey is to return to the Nile, the waters of life, for Menelaus 'omitted to make due sacrifice ... before the journey began.' That sacrifice is the recognition that we who are born will some-day die, yet such knowledge is life-giving.

How long does grief last? When does Proteus turn into this Tree of Life? Each person's grief is unique and depends both on the nature of the relationship we had with the person who has died and our willingness to complete our relationship to the pain of grief. Nevertheless, Grief also carries people in her arms, the twins of Love and Compassion. At the end of the journey we are gifted with a love for the one who has died at a deeper level and we are more open to compassion for others who find themselves in similar situations. With such knowledge to inform and invigorate us, we can move forward once more into the realm of living beings. Then and only then have we learned the truth of grief: only after we have lain down with the seals can we understand that loss is a fundamental and necessary part of human life that we need to experience in order to live fully in this present moment, and that there is life to be lived after grief has come to call.

* * *

Notes

1.   Homer, *The Odyssey*, trans. E. V. Rieu (Harmondsworth: Penguin Books, 1946), pp. 73-77.

1
What is Grief?

Death ends a life, not a relationship.
- Morrie Schwartz (1916-1995)

In the eighteenth century Benjamin Franklin stated that there were only two certainties in life: death and taxes. In truth, the two things that are most certain in life are death and time. Death and time are the two great immutables we encounter in the turmoil of human life: we live in time and we will die in time, and thus somewhere along this timescape, we will experience a person intimately involved with our life removed from it with resounding finality.

Time is the most precious commodity we have. We often spend it striving for what we think will make us happy and working in a job that pays the rent or mortgage, little understanding that the seemingly unproductive times we spend with those we love nourish us just as much on an inner level. Since time moves us inexorably towards death, therefore, it is death that we must make our ally in order to understand that time is limited. The way this is made clear to us is through the emotion of grief, since grief awakens us to death.

The fear of death and the experience of grief are two sides of the coin called loss. Homer was one of the first to encapsulate this overwhelming and primal response.[1] In Chapter XVIII of *The Iliad* entitled 'Armour for Achilles', he wrote:

King Nestor's son halted before him with the hot tears pouring down his cheeks and gave him the lamentable news: 'Alas, my royal lord Achilles! I have a dreadful thing to tell you - I would to God it were not true. Patroclus has been killed. They are fighting round his naked corpse and Hector of the flashing helmet has your arms.'

When Achilles heard this he sank into the black depths of despair. He picked up the dark dust in both hands and poured it on his head. He soiled his comely face with it, and filthy ashes settled on his scented tunic. He cast himself down on the earth and lay there like a fallen giant, fouling his hair and tearing it out with his own hands. The maidservants whom he and Patroclus had captured caught the alarm and all ran screaming out of doors. They beat their breasts with their hands and sank to the ground beside their royal master.

On the other side, Antilochus shedding tears of misery held the hands of Achilles as he sobbed out his noble heart for fear that he might take a knife and cut his throat.[2]

Grief can be defined as the emotional response to loss and the process of adjustment to a new situation. Grief occurs when familiar patterns of behaviour end or change and in so doing, cause conflicting emotions.[3] If someone you love has been ill and in physical pain for a long time, there may be a sense of relief at their death. There will also be sorrow at not being able to continue that relationship and, possibly, fear of the future. A woman in her seventies who has been married for forty or fifty years may, during her husband's protracted illness, secretly yearn for the time when her spouse dies in order to gain her freedom, only to find upon his death that she is overwhelmed by the distress of the loss and immobilized with fear at stepping out alone into her own life.

Mal McKissock, one of Australia's best known and respected bereavement counsellors and educators, defined the difference between bereavement and grief in this way:

> Linguistically, bereavement is the condition, and grief is the emotional experience of it... grief therefore would be a response to almost any sort of loss, whereas bereavement defines one sort of loss. So how you react in your bereavement will be your grief. So that's why people grieve, but they don't bereave.[4]

Grief belongs to all of us and, whether we like it or not, it is the universal signal that life's beat will never again be the same, that the solid rock upon which we once stood is now a passage to an uncertain future. In our lifetime any one of us will experience a variety of losses: the death of a relative, divorce, moving home, job loss, loss of limb, and so on. Whilst responses to these losses share a similar form, it is generally agreed that loss through death is the most significant, perhaps because its finality forces us to confront our own mortality.

Statistics tell us that once every nine-to-thirteen years we will lose someone close to us through death and, assuming we come from a family where we know both parents, then at least twice in our lifetime we will make funeral arrangements for someone we love. In the USA, approximately nine million people out of a population of 328 million have first-time encounters with loss and bereavement from death each year.[5] In the UK, 607,000 deaths were registered in 2017, leaving an estimated 1.2 million out of a population of 66 million facing a major bereavement.[6]

Grief is exhausting, complex and confusing. Faced with the end of an intimate relationship built on connection and togetherness, how we live in the world as a single entity can seem alien and difficult to comprehend and as we attempt to integrate this experience into our life and sort out a new relationship with the person who has died, we will often feel swamped with child-like reactions and vulnerable in a way that is bewildering. As a result, this process of adjustment takes time; indeed, it is not uncommon for it to last up to five years, not as a linear ongoing state, but tidal and cyclic in its cast. This tells us a significant fact, that whilst loss through death may be an uncommon occurrence in our personal lives, if every thirteen years or so we encounter a major loss and the grief process takes around five years to unravel, then thirty percent of our life may be spent dealing with some degree of loss. Hence it is likely that thirty percent of your friends will be going through this process also. In some manner, shape or form, they will be lying down with the seals.

Grief makes us wiser, less innocent and develops our inherent resilience. It is a part of life, an experience we will all encounter. In Shakespeare's *Troilus and Cressida* (3.3.163-169), Ulysses recognizes that death brings us all to equality when he cries:

> O let not virtue seek
> Remuneration for the thing it was;
> For beauty, wit,
> High birth, vigour of bone, desert in service,

Love, friendship, charity, are subjects all
To envious and calumniating time.
One touch of nature makes the whole world kin…[7]

Yet few people plan for it and 53% of the UK population
have not made a will.[8] Instead we live as a death-denying
society that prefers to believe that science, which separates
us from the natural processes of life, has all the answers.
Couple that with a medical profession that views the loss
of life as a failure, the demands of advertising with its
mandate to look and stay young and the fast-disappearing
rituals of life, and we end up with a society unconsciously
believing that ageing and death are to be feared. The spate
of young women taking anabolic steroids in order to lose
weight fast as part of their gym training programme, or
young men obsessed with their body image and their
fixation with building muscle, is as much alarming for
the physical side effects (edginess and irritability, panic
attacks and palpitations, hair loss, acne, deepening of the
voice, growth of body hair and shrinking of the breasts,
as well as an increase in blood pressure, and kidney, heart,
and liver damage) as for the underlying reasons for taking
them. Nancy, a (then) twenty-five-year old woman from
New York, said after taking steroids for six months that she
would continue to take them for her athletic femininity
and improved sex life, and because 'this summer will be
my best yet because I am twenty-five and I don't look a
day over eighteen.'[9] Is it any wonder that when we come
to face loss through death, we have few tools to handle the
separation and isolation and believe that within a week,
two weeks or three weeks after the funeral we should start
to feel better?

Once, death was an integral part of extended family life and bereaved people were supported by family and friends. The Romans thought death should be kept in mind at all times, especially when life at its peak might make one forget the other, equally necessary part of the cycle. When a military hero entered Rome in triumphal procession, riding in a golden chariot, hailed as a god, a person wearing the mask and costume of Death stood at his shoulder, preserving him from the sin of hubris by whispering in his ear, 'Man, remember you will die.' Today our experience of death is lonelier for, as a society, we tend to live as couples or on our own and put our parents into residential care when they grow old, so they can be given appropriate nursing and medical attention. The price we pay for this is the loss of intimacy and the opportunity to share in their last moments of life. Our society is one where the living have become isolated from the dying. In 2003 the Grief Recovery Institute, USA, conducted a survey and asked: 'What is the best way to act around someone who has just experienced the death of a loved one?' From the multiple choice answers, ninety-eight percent of the respondents chose, 'Act as if nothing had happened.' Of those who had experienced such a loss in the past five years they asked, 'In the weeks and months immediately following the death of your loved one, what did you most want and need to do?' Ninety-four percent responded, 'Talk about what happened and my relationship with the person who died.'

If we are not allowed to verbalise or handle these issues as they arise, if the immediate need to understand the excruciating pain by talking about it does not have a clear channel in which to run, how can we find ways to make sense of what is happening to us? If we block what is most urgent inside us, it develops into a spur, silently, invisibly, endlessly pulling on our energy, forcing us to dodge from life. How can we stop this? The truth is always simple: all relationships exist on the assumption that we have endless time. When death cuts a swathe through that belief, we have nowhere to go with the unfinished plans of the relationship, the conversations we still want to have, the hours of love-making that now will never be, the actions and intentions that have no room to flower. If we can discover the nature of these truncated concerns — the actions we still want to take, the things we wished we'd said and the things we regretted saying — then the grief will be whole. By discovering what is incomplete in the relationship, we are able to say goodbye to the shock and the pain of the separation and remember instead the love and warmth, the joy and exhilaration that existed between us. In this way we can begin to build a new emotional and spiritual relationship with our beloved for the rest of our lives.

Death brings irrevocable change. Grief is its response.
Irrevocable changes come in many forms, not just through death, but also from encounters with birth, sex, and handling money and shared resources. These are all issues western society finds difficult to handle, for they force us into situations from which we emerge forever altered. This is learned knowledge, acquired through interaction. Women do not automatically know how to give birth, nor men how to support their partner in so doing and it is now common practice in the West for both partners in an expectant birth

situation to attend ante-natal classes. Initially we fumble with sexual technique and if we are lucky to have a partner who takes the time to explore this domain with us, we gain sexually fulfilling lives. We do not, as a matter of course, know how to handle money and many a person in low-income conditions who wins the lottery has, within a short period of time, lost that money. We are, however, forced to invest time explaining the monies we have earned each year so we can pay taxes. Why do we not, as a society, do the same annual inventory for emotional change? Instead we are forced to pretend that death does not exist and that grief will never touch us. If we treated our taxes in the same way as we treated loss, we would be thrown into prison and the financial economy of the country would grind to a halt.

Until the early twenty-first century no-one had seriously considered that there was such a thing as the emotional economy of a country, nor that it could, in any way, be connected with loss and grief. In November, 2002, The Grief Recovery Institute, USA, published the results of the 25,000 interviews it had conducted in North America in its (then) twenty-five years of operation. Almost all the people interviewed said their job performance was affected by grief. Using conservative estimates and assuming that the death of a loved one produced just one primary mourner who, over the next two years, lost a total of thirty days of productivity, the Grief Index, the term used by the Institute for measuring the hidden annual costs of grief in America's workplace, indicated that the minimum annual effect for U.S. businesses in lost productivity and on-the-job errors was $37.6 billion.[10] Given that workplace grief includes not only the death of a loved one, but also divorce/marital problems, family crisis, death of an acquaintance, money issues at home and pet loss, the study estimates that hidden grief costs U.S. companies more than $75 billion annually in reduced productivity, increased errors and accidents. As a statement of how little consideration is given to grief and workplace behaviour, no other industry groups, including those representing funeral directors, hospices and others that monitor and study grief, had any comparable statistics. Three days used to be the typical amount of time given for bereavement leave throughout corporate America. A survey by The Society for Human Resource Management, an organization for human resource executives, showed that ninety-two percent of companies offered paid bereavement leave for four days or fewer and sixty-eight percent of businesses said they have employee-assistance programs for people in grief, up from sixty four percent in 1999.[11] The Grief Recovery Institute, USA, advocates ten days bereavement leave and encourages grief breaks for employees, such as a walk outside or a talk with a co-worker, to allow them to be more productive the rest of the day. The aims of The Grief Recovery Institute are admirable and designed to help businesses gain greater awareness of the needs of people in grief, yet it is also a reflection of society that they have had to use the only model the business world understands: one that is mechanistic and reductionist and thus equates a human being to an automaton whose productivity is diminished by loss. Needing to convert the human emotion of grief into dollars and cents is a statement of how little business understands how to deal with grief in the workplace.

For all that, it is wise not be too harsh on the commercial world. Since major emotional losses are not regular occurrences in our lives, few people have any preparation for handling grief or are equipped to support family and friends at times of personal loss. We are only given relevant information about how to deal with funerals in the days following the death and, more often than not, it is left to the funeral director and the medical practitioner to help people deal with the cascade of emotions. Here is an example. In *The Eye* magazine of 10-16 January, 2004, television screenwriter Paul Abbott described his impoverished childhood. Born second to last of ten children, his mother left without explanation when he was nine. His father became an alcoholic and abandoned the family to the care of the eldest sibling, a pregnant seventeen year old, when Abbott was eleven. At the age of fifteen Abbott attempted suicide. He became 'a ward niner', the term used for the local psychiatric facility and in this black hole of destitution, he determined he would turn his life around. He was fostered and then went to Manchester University to study psychology, leaving after two years when a play he'd written was performed on Radio 4. Now happily married, he has a much better relationship with his father whom he describes as 'a reformed character, adored by his grandchildren'. It was a different story when his mother died. 'I felt nothing,' he said. 'We went to the funeral, but it ended up with a brawl between two of my brothers. I think everyone was confused about what they were meant to feel.'

We prefer to bypass trying to grapple with these feelings until it is necessary, yet our lives are full of loss experiences that produce the same feelings of grief: the death of an animal friend, moving house and home, starting school, changes to one's health, graduating from high school, university or a place of extended learning, divorce, retirement, and the absence of children when they leave home. Since they are not identified as circumstances which produce grief in the same way as death, we pay little attention to how they can teach us to deal with major losses when they occur. Furthermore, if any of these losses are emotionally significant to us and are not dealt with appropriately at the time, then, like mineral salts in hard water, they build up as unresolved issues that accumulate over time and influence how we will respond to the death of a loved one in the future. How has this come to be?

Acquisition versus letting go

Any capitalistic society is an acquisitive society. From an early age we are taught to look outwards and to acquire things, emotionally as well as physically: our parents' love and respect, a good education, a job, a house, car and family of our own. No-one teaches us what to do when things pass out of our lives, or when the goals we set are not achieved. No-one teaches us the true meaning of feelings of failure and despair. In his introduction to *The Prayer Tree*, Australian cartoonist and philosopher Michael Leunig wrote:

> Nature requires that we form a relationship between our joy and our despair, that they not remain divided or hidden from one another. For these are the feelings which must cross-pollinate and inform each other in order that the soul be enlivened and strong.
>
> It is the soul, after all, which bears the burden of our experience. It is the soul through which we love and it is the soul which senses most faithfully our function within the integrity of the natural world.[12]

Every loss, every death we encounter, throws us into winter, into that shapeless void in which poet John Keats so elegantly stated, no birds sing and the sedge is withered from the lake. 'I knew that I had moved inexplicably and without return from the white squares of the tiles on my kitchen floor onto the black squares when my mother died,' remarked a friend. Grief lives in the fade out between the old season which dies and before spring arrives, 'the night that lies between two days'.[13] Grief is symbolised by the balsamic 'dark moon' phase of any cycle, offering release without replacement. You can see the balsamic Moon each month in the sky, the thin sliver of the dying moon once full and glorious with luminous sun, now dark against the growing pre-dawn light, outlining the shape and the shadow of what has been, a transcript of the vital processes of the previous month now concluded. The balsamic phase is the phase of letting go, when life clears a space for us to reprioritise our life without immediately filling it with people and events. Often such action is accompanied by panic, since from an early age, we are taught Replacement Theory:

Breakdown = Substitute or Replace

We learn this by observing how our parents reacted to change in the material world: when the washing machine, which laboured for years in the sweaty drudge of cleaning our clothes, stopped working they called in someone to repair it or bought another; when the car broke down, they called for road service or traded it in for a new one. Nowadays obsolescence is often deliberately built into motor-driven items such as electric toothbrushes and vacuum cleaners. We are encouraged to see household goods as short-term and to replace them when they burn out. This made sense with domestic appliances, but Replacement Theory also cascaded into emotional territory when our parents encouraged us to eat something when we were upset, rather than deal with the excruciating pain of being shunned or excluded in some way and to solve that first, before substituting those emotions. The same applies to our audio environment. In our daily lives it is rare to walk into a shop that does not bombard us with raucous music or talkback radio, drowning the opportunity to hear our own thoughts and to make considered judgements, relying instead on advertising to unconsciously drive us. It is a potent combination: we refuse to allow the mechanics of our life to stop us from moving forward and we learn to replace silence and space with noise. So when personal relationships and intimate connections 'break down', we have a ready-made template built from years of Replacement Theory to apply to the situation. It takes time to understand our own motivations and time to appreciate another's motivations in a relationship.

Relationship dynamics change as people change; there is no blame in this. Sometimes we simply outgrow each other and different pathways beckon us across a growing gulf. Nevertheless, we are not taught how to deal with the often-enormous emotional cost of the end of a living relationship, let alone one that is severed by death. Any separation, no matter how amicable, will cause feelings of rejection, isolation, and emotional pain. This is an extremely painful place in which to exist. 'Our species brings to it the capacity for self-reflexive awareness and responsible acts,' wrote social critic and ecofeminist Charlene Spretnak.[14] Yet apart from the first few days after a loved one dies, the extended family is usually no longer physically around to support and help a person in grief and in the precious few days when they are, our culture has determined what sort of behaviour is acceptable — behaviour which does not necessarily relate to the needs of the bereaved. Achilles' reaction would not be tolerated if he received Patroclus' news today and yet his response in that moment was the healthiest thing he could have done.

There are two ways to avoid grief in human life: the first is to die young, before anyone you love precedes you. In 1989 I had the privilege of working with young people from the depressed western suburbs of Adelaide, South Australia. I was their playwright-in-residence, working with them to create a play about youth and alcohol. The catch cry amongst their difficult and straitened lives was: 'Die young, stay pretty'. The second way to prevent grief is to avoid ever really loving or caring for someone. That way you never have to be emotionally involved with death or its consequences. Grief is the price we pay for living a full life. If we think of a life as a complete picture, when we lose a loved one it is as if that picture crazes, like a jigsaw puzzle, and some of the pieces fall out. Most people do not take steps to recover those pieces, so unconsciously we carry a fragmentary image around inside us, believing we are still whole. These empty spaces accumulate over time and when we next encounter loss, without realising it more pieces of the puzzle fall out. Unless we pay attention to these lost fragments, we walk around as incomplete puzzles our whole life. These buried or forgotten losses extend the pain and frustration of how to deal with letting go. This is unresolved grief and it becomes our learned response to the world. Honouring Replacement Theory, unconsciously we look for people to fill those spaces for us. Such unconscious projections can create explosive situations when we encounter loss as an adult.

Is grief a terminal illness?

Any discussion about loss and grief must inevitably bring up the name of Elisabeth Kübler-Ross, the brilliant pioneer who worked in the field of death and dying. Her contribution has been invaluable and has, in many ways, profoundly affected the manner in which the medical profession deals with terminally ill patients. Through her decisive and shaping work begun in 1965 and outlined in her book, *On Death and Dying*, Kübler-Ross identified five emotional stages that a person experiences when they have been diagnosed with a terminal illness, namely:

Stage 1: denial by the person and isolation from other people.

Stage 2: anger, rage, envy and resentment of those who are still able to live and function.

Stage 3: bargaining to postpone the inevitable event and extend the person's life.

Stage 4: depression, both reactive to the loss of lifestyle and preparatory for the death.

These stages then become the stepping stones towards…

Stage 5: acceptance.

These stages do not replace each other. Rather they exist next to each other and at times overlap. No matter what the stage of the illness or the mechanisms used to handle it, all terminally ill patients maintain hope right until the last moment. Kübler-Ross developed these stages at a time when modern thinking had reached its peak with its emphasis on rationalism and functionality. She established the system as a psychiatrist for thanatological purposes (the scientific study of death) to help the terminally ill die with grace and dignity whilst having their needs met. Later she applied her work to large groups of terminally ill people outside the hospital environment, as well as to members of the family connected with the dying and published her work under titles which underlined the work she did: *Death: The Final Stage of Growth*; *On Children and Death*; and *Working It Through*. In *To Live Until We Say Goodbye* Kübler-Ross wrote:

> With her favourite music playing, with candlelight on the table, with her children near, and with flowers next to her picked by her own children, she died a very different kind of death than had she stayed in the hospital. Those children will never associate death with loneliness, isolation, playing games and deceit. They will remember it as a time of togetherness with their parents and grandparents, and friends who cared and were able to acknowledge their own anxieties and their own fears, and together were able to overcome them.[15]

Counsellors and therapists, the clergy and the medical profession working in the field of bereavement, influenced by the revelations of Kübler-Ross's investigations and the lack of work done in this taboo area, chose to apply the concept of these stages of dying to the grief that follows death. This occurred because it fitted into a medical model which treated grief as an illness and bereavement as a disease. This linear way of seeing the world moved from diagnosis to prognosis, treatment, and, finally, to intervention. Thus 'stages' meant that people could predict moments in time and, as a result, tell grieving people whether they were moving through them as quickly as they should, inferring that the stages were sequential and predictable. People, however, are complicated, irrational and emotional and their responses to grief are neither sequential nor predictable. Practitioners forgot that Kübler-Ross's work was carried out in the field of the dying and that her overlapping, co-existent 'stages' applied to someone who knew that the end point of their present life was death. The process of grief is the antithesis of this. The word 'grief' comes from Old French 'grever' meaning burden or encumber, in turn based on the Latin 'gravare', from 'gravis' meaning heavy, grave. In Middle English the word also means to harm or oppress. The process of grief is learning how to free oneself from the pain of the loss, pain that can become a burden if not resolved, removing the harm that can come from not dealing with what has happened. The end point of grief is life, to live again when one has been awakened to death.

In the same way as architecture in the 1970s changed its tone from modern to postmodern, railing against functionality and demanding respect for the structures of social relationships that make homes and communities flow better, so the perception of grief has undergone a sea change. People working in the field of bereavement now recognise that human beings grieve according to unpredictable dependent variables which include age, gender, day of the week, how close a person was emotionally to the one who died, and the nature of the death. They also recognise that the quality, strength, passion, and the force of feelings that overwhelm us after a death reflect the quality, strength, passion and the force of feelings of the relationship. McKissock likened grief to chaos theory which, he said, reflected his experience of counselling people in grief in clinical practice. In brief, one can think of chaos theory as the mechanics of studying nonlinear, dynamic systems which are mathematically deterministic, and nearly impossible to predict. McKissock suggested that the effect grief had on people and how they dealt with it could not be described by logical, linear systems or pathways and that a person in grief was better off responding to what was happening to them in the moment, rather than according to what should be happening.

A better model might be the still-evolving complexity theory, a refinement of chaos theory. Complexity is the observed tendency of seemingly random agents to arrange themselves into patterns. This zone, known as the edge of chaos, lies between inertia and anarchy and is thought to be the place where evolution is most likely to occur. Mitchell Waldrop defined complexity as 'a class of behaviours in which the components of the system never quite lock into place, yet never quite dissolve into turbulence, either.'[16] As human beings, we respond in the same way. When confronted with disruption or complex systems, we move towards creating ordered patterns or, if life is gridlocked and jammed over a period of time, then there is a high probability that it will erupt into pandemonium. Applying complexity theory to grief, then, the initial pain, distress and agony catapults a person into chaos. In such a state a person will focus all their energy to fight, scrabble, heave, tug and claw their way back to the regular matrix of ordered life — just as Menelaus struggled with Proteus. What they encounter on their return, however, is not the world they knew. Grief is a passage which leads to a changed future. If a person can surrender to the grief, then life initially seems chaotic, but eventually settles back to the resilient patterns we call equilibrium. If grief is repressed, it pushes a person into stasis, an immobilised state where they can remain for years, becalmed in the bay like Menelaus. Then, complexity theory suggests, eventually the person's life will erupt into chaos before they can return to a state of equilibrium. The longer a system stays in stasis, the more the movement out of it is through turmoil. Grief spontaneously throws a person into a period of disorder before order returns. We can delay it through repression, but we can't avoid it. To reach the structure of a changed future, we have to go through chaos. Waldrop described it in this way:

> ... we are made of the same elemental compositions, so we are a part of this thing that is never changing and always changing. If you think you are a steamboat and can go up the river, you're kidding yourself. Actually, you're just the captain of a paper boat drifting down the river. If you try to resist, you're not going to get anywhere. On the other hand, if you quietly observe the flow, realising that you are part of it, realising that the flow is ever-changing and always leading to new complexities, then every so often you can stick an oar into the river and punt yourself from one eddy to another.[17]

Only now is the world of science catching up with what the ancients knew so long ago, that as Menelaus, in the myth of grief, struggled with The Old Man of the Sea, so he was propelled into disarray and chaos. All he could do was to hold onto Proteus and be catapulted through the maelstrom of grief, for it is this maelstrom which awakened him to death and which, eventually, allowed him to sail home to the safety of the edge of chaos and a changed world.

Rites of passage

Grief is a rite of passage and all rites of passage contain paradoxes: they celebrate changes and disruptions in a seemingly continuous life; and they acknowledge the fact that we are born and die alone, yet as a group we seek to find meaning in events which define birth, ageing, and death. While paradoxes can never be resolved, the in-built framework and safeguards that rituals provide allow us to experience their truth. It was Arnold van Gennep, the twentieth-century pioneer in the structure of rites of passage who, in 1907, observed that a person or a group of people had to be separated from one role or rank in society before he, she or they could be incorporated into a new one. In this liminal phase between the two positions something extraordinary occurred. Native cultures employed sleep-deprivation and fasting to induce the extremes of emotional and physical stress and at the end of this transitional time, the individual or group of people emerged rejuvenated and was welcomed back into the community in a new role.

Building on van Gennep's work, British cultural anthropologist Victor Turner found that people who were in this liminal phase were not only out of place in the ordered structure of society, they became mysterious and powerful as they underwent change. Historian of religion Mircea Eliade suggested that rituals, along with myths,

gave us access to sacred or cyclic time.[18] Paralleling this
was the work of Joseph Campbell, the American writer on
mythology and comparative religion, who discovered that
the journeys all central characters took in the great myths of
the world contained three major phases: departure from the
known world; initiation through isolation and encounters
with dangerous elements; and the return to the tribe or
the common world with a gift that would help those who
had stayed behind. Given that journeys were undertaken
to bring about change, this journey of adjustment and
growth forged strength of character. This voyage had its
price, however, for, as Campbell noted, '… every one of us
shares the supreme ordeal … not in the bright moments of
his tribe's great victories but in the silences of his personal
despair.'[19] Despair, it seems, is a necessary component of
the ritual in order to catalyse change.

Rites of passage occur whenever we encounter life
crises. They create anxiety by calling attention to seemingly
irreconcilable human paradoxes. They shake us out of our
mundane way of being, with our previous ways of acting,
thinking and feeling and, separated from society, provide
us with a new context for learning from which we emerge
forever changed. The world is undone and the world
is made new again. The same can be said of grief, yet in
today's modern, industrial world where individuality is
prized, the cost is often experiencing life's transitions alone.
We are, for the most part, born in hospitals and that is
where most of us can expect to die. Birth and death are
the two great portals of our lives, yet so often they are left
unsanctified and uncelebrated. Grief, the hitchhiker on the
same pathway as death, becomes not so much the great
reflector of transition, but an illness or sickness of which

no-one speaks. Grief's shape shares this pattern:

> • **Acute grief** — the initial response, where we are ripped from the world of common day and thrust into the turmoil and despair of grief;
>
> • **Disintegration** — the period of disengagement from the world where we discover that the rules we have developed for living in the mundane world do not work in the land of grief and the mist in our head and the pain in our heart seldom clears;
>
> • **Reintegration** back into the community after a passage of time, but now in a new and productive role.

This pattern can also be expressed as a mandorla.

Grief as a Mandorla

When two opposing forces come into conflict with each other, a unique space called a *mandorla* — the space between two opposing elements — is created. *Mandorla* is the Italian word for almond. This ancient symbol appears in the images and myths of cultures around the world, from the Igbo people of West Africa to the old Celtic tribes of Europe. These earliest shapes symbolically represented the mysterious feminine aspect of life as a sacred womb, a portal between the realm of spirit and the realm of matter, through which all life passes into this world. Also known as the *Vesica Piscis*, symbolizing the interactions and interdependence of opposing worlds and forces, the mandorla demonstrates that opposites overlap and are finally the same.[20] The space within the overlap is the place in which we are asked to stay whilst change occurs. This is a threshold or liminal space, a space that occupies both sides of a boundary, the place at which you arrive after you leave one room and have not yet entered another. Living on such thresholds requires faith, for all change takes place in liminal space. Robert Johnson wrote of this in *Owning Your Own Shadow*:

> Whenever you have a clash of opposites in your being and neither will give way to the other... you can be certain that God is present.
>
> We dislike this experience intensely and avoid it at any cost. But if we can endure it, the conflict-without-resolution is a direct experience of God.... the space between these two opposing elements is a place of healing.[21]

The idea, wrote Johnson, is that gradually the two spaces overlap to become one so that there is no longer the separation between me and my shadow self or that which is projected outwards and unowned. If one of the circles is us and the other our encounter with the death of a beloved, then the mandorla is the space of grief.

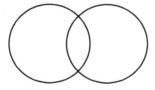

With consciousness, gradually the two spaces overlap to become one, so that finally the separation no longer exists between me and the one who has died. Instead there is the realisation of a newer level of awareness where the memory of the other is contained and absorbed within us in a different way.

The shape of grief

Grief pummels us from within, unplugging what was previously a highly active and capable intellectual capacity and leaving only pure emotion. Whilst everyone's grief is unique and our personal expression of it depends on the relationship we had with the person who has died, the emotional and physical responses which wash over and around us are remarkably uniform:

Shock and numbness

Grief is an emotional wound. It causes pain in the same way as a physical wound. The body's response when we first hear of the death of a loved one is to produce powerful, pain-killing drugs similar to heroin and morphine known as enkephalins and met-enkephalins. These endorphins are natural narcotic-like chemicals produced at the level the body needs.[22] If you have ever jammed your thumb in a door or cut yourself with a knife, you will experience the same rush of chemical activity on a vastly reduced scale. This numbing effect is designed to enable the person to take action. A gashed leg, a wounded arm, a jammed thumb, all of these require attention immediately and our own natural pain-killers give us the time to attend to the wound, make a phone call for help or take action in some way. In such circumstances there is usually only a short delay before the pain comes rushing back. It is not so with grief. This numbness that a person feels, this lack of physical or emotional sensation — and sometimes it is both — is often misinterpreted as denial but is, in reality, shock. Shock is the sudden disruption to our daily routines which causes a distressing effect on the mind and feelings and initiates suffering. Shock occurs whenever we experience pain or life-threatening situations. The associated numbness is one of a range of physical responses designed to decrease the immediate pain until it can be managed, and it can last for hours, days and sometimes months.

Fear

Fear is an emotion triggered by the belief that someone or something is dangerous and likely to create pain. Fear causes our pulse to race and our blood to pump faster. It prepares us for fight or flight. Its origin is the Old English word 'fær' meaning calamity or danger and 'færan' meaning frighten, as well as reverence of the numinous. It is thought to be the first functional response to have evolved as part of the autonomic nervous system five hundred million years ago and it is as potent today as it was for our prehistoric ancestors.[23] When someone we love dies, fear of the future and fear of not being able to deal with the huge emotional and physical change that has just entered our life are normal and natural responses. Such fears are designed to pinpoint areas in a person's life that have dramatically altered in order for the person to reset the parameters of their life. A reduction of financial income, for example, may be a real fear if the person has been relying on his or her partner to supply the weekly wages. Other fears may have little grounding in reality, yet impose an even greater emotional threat, such as the fear of living life without the partner. Although they may evoke panic, concern and worry, fears once named can be managed and the person in grief needs space to voice these concerns. We have, however, been socialized to express fear indirectly as rage, revenge or self-loathing and these can have long-term consequences if they are allowed to define the person's life. Uncontrolled fear can be the underlying cause of anxiety disorders and some of the symptoms of depression.

Anger

Anger is a natural, adaptive response to threats. It inspires powerful, often aggressive, feelings and behaviours which allow us to fight and to defend ourselves when we are attacked. Like other emotions, it is accompanied by physiological and biological changes. When we get angry, our heart rate and blood pressure rise, as do the levels of our energy hormones, adrenalin and noradrenalin. A certain amount of anger is necessary for our survival, but anger can vary in intensity from mild irritation to intense fury and rage, any of which can be triggered by external and/or internal events, such as a person, an event or concern with a personal problem. Memories of traumatic or enraging events can also release angry feelings. In the case of grief, anger may sometimes be associated with the circumstances of the loss. When someone has been prevented from being with the person when they died, they may experience anger at the turn of events. Katrina told me this experience regarding her father's death:

> In November 1993, I left for a three-month trip to the Far East, partially motivated by a desire to consider some changes in my life. Not long before I left, my father had said to me that his desire was that I would be happy and I had the sense that he knew I was not entirely happy in the field in which I was working. In December, when I was in Nepal, I had a dream that

my father came to me and told me that he had died.
I thought at that moment that I should call home,
but didn't want to upset my mother. However, about
two days later I was walking in the street and had a
profound urge to call home and I did. My mother and
my brother were just leaving the house for the funeral,
having desperately tried to contact me in Nepal, but
to no avail because I was in transit when the event
occurred. My father's death was unexpected, caus-
ing a deep emotional wound that motivated me to
change my career and go back to school on my return
to Canada. Given the circumstances of the dream, I
was not angry that I only found out about my father's
death on the day of his funeral. In fact, I was relieved
that I found out in the manner I did, seeing as my
mother was having such a hard time contacting me.
What I was particularly angry about is that, just when
I felt I had found some freedom, I was suddenly decidedly restricted because I knew that when I went back
to Canada, my responsibilities to my mother would
be increased manifold. This was a most painful and
confusing time because, just as I was liberated from
one restriction, I was facing another. On the surface,
this might sound callous, but my relationship with
my mother was exceedingly difficult, owing to her
alcoholism throughout my childhood. So, yes, I was
immensely angry because I felt that, just as I was beginning to fly, my wings were clipped or perhaps they
melted because I got too close to the sun.

If the relationship has been blocked or stifled in any way,
then the person may be angry that the one they loved
has died before they have had a chance to mend the

relationship. In such instances anger is often displaced onto a 'safe' family member. Here's an example. Alan lived in a different city from his father. In the midst of a telephone conversation, he became angry at his father, swore at him and hung up. A month later his father died. Alan's initial reaction to his father's death was: 'I'm not ready for this!' Two months later, in another telephone conversation, his younger brother confronted him with their mother's now-restricted financial income. Alan's parents had both been retired and living on pensions. They had lost their family home many years earlier through bankruptcy and Alan and his wife had taken it upon themselves to buy his parents a small flat. He had used his parents' pension to help pay off the mortgage. He had not, however, thought to put them on the title deed alongside himself as security of tenure in their old age. Despite these changed events, he still assumed that his mother would continue to contribute to the rates on her now-halved pension. His younger brother suggested that Alan take on board a standard landlord's responsibilities and pay the rates himself. Alan became enraged at what he thought was his younger brother's disrespectful way of treating him. He demanded an apology and when his younger brother refused, Alan swore at him and slammed the phone down. In a letter he threatened to cut off all connection with his younger brother unless the apology was forthcoming. His younger brother maintained his position and Alan held onto his anger for five years as a way of preventing him from confronting the pain of loss and the guilt of his last actions towards his father. In the course of my interview with him, Alan came to the painful realisation that he had duplicated the circumstances of his last conversation with his father with his younger brother.

At first he had tried to vindicate his actions and when that did not work, he had displaced his anger onto this safe member of his family until he was ready to look at it. The circumstances preceding the loss of Alan's father had been unresolved and so he experienced anger. Anger, however, is not an automatic part of grief.

Reduced concentration

'No-one ever told me about the laziness of grief,' wrote C.S. Lewis.[24] 'Not only writing but even reading a letter is too much.' The reactions of someone in grief are slower than normal. A person's entire being in its emotional, physical, and spiritual manifestation is trying to make sense of this painful situation. Lapses in concentration, such as walking into a supermarket without being conscious of how one has arrived there, or making a phone call without being aware of picking up the telephone and dialling, are the hallmarks of this natural friend of acute grief. This inability to concentrate can be such a profound state that one should avoid driving or working with tools that require concentration and mental co-ordination in the immediate aftermath of a death, since this is when a high percentage of serious and often fatal accidents occur.

Being tearful

Tears play a vital role in our visual system. Physically the lachrymal gland of the eyes produces aqueous fluid in response to a sensation of dryness or irritation. These are called continuous or basal tears. Reflex tears or irritant tears are those which spring to our eyes in response to smoke, onion vapours or foreign bodies. They are produced by tiny glands on the underside of the upper eyelid and drain through a nasolacrimal duct into the nose where they are reabsorbed. When tears run down the face, it is because there are too many of them to drain. Tears are an efficient cleaning medium, washing foreign bodies from the eye and providing microbiological protection. They also produce a high quality optical surface which forms the major light-refracting element of the eye. Since the cornea has no blood vessels, nutrients and waste products are transported to and from it via the surface tear film. Tears contain immunoglobulins and enzymes that protect the eye from infection. They contain oils and mucus that form a thin film which protects the surface of the eye.[25]

Continuous tears and reflex tears are fairly well understood and occur in other animals. Yet apart from a few reports in animals — an Indian elephant, an African gorilla, female seals, some species of dogs and others — humans are believed to be the only animals that shed tears when they are overwhelmed by intense emotion. We cry when we are joyful, in grief or despondent, tormented by hopelessness or overwhelmed with relief. We cry when exhilarated or creased over with laughter, when brimming with pride or beyond the limits of sheer ecstasy. We cry when we stand in front of paintings.[26] These psychogenic lachrymations reflect the immense range of emotions of which humans are capable. Primal therapists understand that crying can be a cathartic release. Cell biologists know that emotional tears have specific biological pathways, although they still don't know whether they are caused by hormones or chemical messengers from nerves. Indeed, little is known about these tears of emotions.

To explore this further, in the early 1980s, biochemist William H. Frey II screened the films *The Champ*, *Brian's*

Song and *All Mine to Give* and asked a select group of viewers to collect their tears in test tubes. He also collected the reflex tears of people cutting onions. He discovered that emotional tears were chemically different from irritant or reflex tears. Amongst other things, emotional tears contained ACTH, a hormone indictor of stress and the endorphin leucine-enkephalin, part of the family of brain chemicals known as endorphins which are thought to modulate pain sensation. He also found high concentrations of manganese, suggesting that tears remove toxic substances from the blood or other body tissues. Furthermore, Frey found that both emotional and irritant tears contain about thirty times more manganese than is found in blood serum, suggesting that while the lachrymal gland lacks the filtering apparatus of the kidneys, human tear glands can still concentrate and excrete substances from the blood or other body tissues. In sea birds like gulls, albatrosses, and cormorants, and some marine animals, like seals and saltwater crocodiles, tear glands are more powerful than kidneys at removing toxic levels of salt from the body.[27] Frey's conclusion was that something truly unique happens when we shed emotional tears. Tears deal with stress, modulate pain and remove toxic substances, so crying is an appropriate physical response to stress. Indeed most people feel better after crying and regard it as a desirable and healthy release of tension. Mr Bumble in Charles Dickens' *Oliver Twist* understood this when he stated:

> It opens the lungs, washes the countenance, exercises the eyes, and softens down the temper. So cry away![28]

Alfred, Lord Tennyson understood this when, in 1847, he penned in *The Princess*:

> Home they brought her warrior dead.
> She nor swoon'd nor utter'd cry:
> All her maidens, watching, said,
> 'She must weep or she will die.'[29]

Sir Henry Carr Maudsley, physician and pathologist, understood this when in 1918 he wrote: 'The sorrow which has no vent in tears may make other organs weep.'[30] Too many tears, however, smokescreen the powerful depth of feelings that contain the unresolved issues that must be completed with the person who has died. Tears drive a person to the location. It is words, however, that identify what is unspoken in the heart, and lay bare the raw material behind the pain which produces the crying. Psychologist Jeffrey Kottler pointed out that people who are depressed cry all the time and feel worse.[31] Depression is an immobilized state, whereas sadness offers one an acute sense of existence.

For the person in grief, the natural chemicals produced by the body to numb the pain begin to decrease as the weeks pass. Around four-to-six weeks after the death they are significantly low. As these endorphins start to wear off, the full extent of the pain filters through to reality. What seemed manageable before now seems worse than ever. Instead of decreasing, crying may increase as a way of producing more met-enkephalins, utilising the natural chemicals of emotional tears as a way of bringing the body back to a state of balance.

Disrupted sleep patterns

The death of someone close to us is now understood to be one of life's greatest stresses and one of the body's instinctive reactions is to produce adrenalin. This is a chemical secreted by the adrenal glands when the body believes itself to be under threat. It does this in order to provide enough energy to protect itself from danger or to run as far away from the danger as possible: the 'fight or flight' response. Flooding the body with adrenalin creates an increase in blood pressure and heart rate and loads the body's muscles with tension. Think of any athlete on the blocks in the 'get set' position before the gun is fired and you have an understanding of the state of the body at this time: totally primed with no race to run.

In previous generations and in other cultures significant amounts of this adrenalin would have been burned up by mourning, sitting around the body for three days and three nights crying, moaning, screaming and weeping. At the end of this time the person in grief would have been physically exhausted and collapsed with natural fatigue into deep sleep. Our modern western perspective teaches us to placate, patronise or modify such behaviour: 'You must have a good night's sleep. Take a tranquilliser, you'll feel better in the morning'. Medications block the expression of pain. Acute grief is not concerned with feeling better. Indeed, the articulation of feelings, however they come, together with appropriate emotional support, is part of the rite of passage and of primary importance at this time, more so than the need for physical relief. Added to this is the serious side effect of prolonged dependence on the tranquillising qualities of drugs, for habitual use can lead to addiction.

When the doctor informed Clara of her husband's terminal cancer in 1965, she refused to allow anyone to tell her husband that he was dying. When he died suddenly not long afterwards, she began taking the anti-anxiety agent Diazepam (Valium) as a short-term relief to help her sleep. When I interviewed her in 2001 she was still taking half a tablet of Valium every night, totally unable to sleep without it. This was a woman who, after her husband's death, assumed management of his business selling real estate and succeeded as a woman in a man's world. This was a woman who travelled the world extensively, spending a year at a time with her family in Switzerland, her friends in England and her sister-in-law in America. Yet her history of denial of death, her fear of ageing and her refusal to deal with the real and painful loss of her husband had followed her into her old age. When she was eighty and still actively flying around the world, she developed deep vein thrombosis, blood clots in the deep veins of her legs. This led to a series of operations and diminished movement. At the age of eighty five, she had become frail and dependent and continued to be afraid of dying. This was a ripe and opportune time for her to allow those who loved her to deepen their emotional ties to her by participating in her natural process of ageing and, eventually, dying. She, in turn, would gain physical and emotional security as she journeyed forth along that fearful pathway. Instead it resulted in her becoming angry and embittered at her loss of mobility and her vitality, pushing away those who could help her deal with her fears.

Going to bed and sleeping for days at a time or staying awake for long periods of time are natural reactions to acute grief. The body has its own intelligence and will find a balance without the use of medication. Prescribed drugs cloud reality. They may work in the short term, yet as their effects fade, the person's awareness of the pain increases. They are most often prescribed for the sake of someone else rather than to cater for the needs of the person in grief. Indeed bereaved people unconsciously spend most of their time making other people feel better. 'Have an injection/a tablet, it'll help you' in reality translates as: 'We can't handle your emotions. Have an injection/a tablet, it'll help us.'

A more positive expression for this trapped adrenalin is physical exercise such as long walks, swimming, gardening, housework, yoga or having a massage. After the sudden and unexpected death of her father at age seventy, the first of her parents to die, Debbie decided to build a water garden in her back yard, spading the hard earth with her bare hands and installing a clever interconnection of ponds. She planted ferns and flowers around the ponds and added a floodlight and a garden seat for the evenings. The physical activity released her body from feeling continually pumped, the results of her labour gave her an environment from which she received great joy and pleasure, and the end result established a living memorial to her father.

Planting a garden is a common female response to major change and reorganisation and indicative of moving towards a new life. When a person nurtures a garden, it nurtures them back. As seeds shoot into plants and buds into flowers and fruit, so a woman, in effect, midwifes herself into healing. The thirteenth century Persian mystic, Rumi said, 'This outward spring and garden are a reflection of the inward garden.'[32] Contemporary Canadian symbolist painter and writer, Susanne Iles, expressed it this way:

> Plants and flowers, trees and shrubs, have been our
> companions for eons. We grow gardens in our
> backyards, on apartment balconies, rooftops, and
> windowsills. We use plants not only to feed ourselves
> but also to nourish our senses and our connection
> to the earth. Deep within the roots of every plant
> dwell the seeds of myth, waiting to be reclaimed…
> the garden is a sacred place grown from the seeds of
> myth.[33]

Creating her own garden from nothing not only gave
Debbie an outlet for her artistry and vision. The smells,
sounds, colours, textures, and energy of the plants and
trees helped to ground her and ease the intensity of what
was occurring internally.

Changed eating habits

Loss of appetite is a natural reaction to grief, for the body's
energy is directed elsewhere. Feeling ravenous is also a
normal reaction and someone in acute grief may swing
between the two extremes. If this is the case, it is wise to
have ready access to fresh fruit and vegetables, proteins and
carbohydrates, and to drink a plentiful amount of water.

Emotional highs and lows

People explain grief as 'coming in waves' or 'like walking
through hidden swamplands'. One woman described her
feelings as 'like taking an elevator straight from your head
and intellect to your guts and heart'. People in grief find
difficulty in being able to maintain emotional stability
and as a result, will often feel emotionally and physically
drained. Whilst the pain is at first intense and constant,

moments occur where the pain recedes. As these moments increase to hours and then to days, a small and seemingly inconsequential action in the midst of a mundane event can trigger a memory and grief floods back in full three-dimensional colour and pain, as vivid and present as the day it occurred. I heard a man on a talk-back radio station, agitated and distressed. He had just broken a terracotta pot and feelings of rage and guilt were flooding his body. He could not understand what was happening to him, yet twelve months earlier his wife had died and the terracotta pot was the last item they had bought together. Grief is an ever-changing, dynamic process and these are normal and natural reactions.

Bodily distress

Bereavement is a serious traumatic experience. As a result, any bodily system or organ can be affected to a greater or lesser degree. Bodily distresses can range from tightness in the chest or throat, backache and headache, mild gastro-intestinal disturbances such as indigestion, constipation, digestive disorders or heartburn or more incapacitating symptoms such as nausea, vomiting, diarrhoea, menstrual problems, migraine or acute chest pain. One woman found she couldn't stop trembling when her husband died, but reaching out and touching someone would stop the trembling immediately. In this time of stress, the physical body is particularly vulnerable. Coupled with the production of adrenalin, the pituitary gland also produces an immunosuppressant called cortisol which decreases the production of T-lymphocytes, the body's surveillance cells. T-lymphocytes are responsible for keeping infection and other abnormal cells in the body under control. When they are depleted, the body is defined as being immune-suppressed, unable to fight infection or control the production of these abnormal cells. Viruses and bacteria gain the upper hand and the body can succumb to infections such as influenza, cold sores, upper respiratory tract infections, urinary tract infections, boils or conjunctivitis.

Sighing

The weight of grief can seem immense and a common, almost unconscious response is to sigh a great deal. The sigh, this audible exhalation, is the involuntary expression of exhaustion and lament. Deep sighing and frequent swallowing are ways the body releases tension.

'To sleep perchance to dream…'

Are dreams of the dead real contacts or simply images created by the dreamer to meet psychological needs? We will never know. What we do know is that many bereaved people actively dream about the one who has died and those dreams are vibrant, vital and deeply emotional and, in some instances, dramatically alter the way a person views death. At base their effect is healing and the dreamer almost always wakes with a sense of reassurance and exuberance. In the same way that not all people remember their dreams when life moves pleasantly forward in the normal course of events, so not all people in grief remember their dreams. Of those who do dream, however, my interviews showed that early in grief people will experience one of two types of dreams. The first type is a series of dreams in a continuing narrative occurring within the first two-to-three months after the loved one has died. Such dreams include being with them, seeing them or having conversations with them at places of transition which represent the boundaries between the two worlds, such as on a bus or a boat, at a railway station, a wharf or an airport, by a door or gate, in a hallway or a tunnel. The final dream in the series usually occurs with the person who has died leaving for a distant land. The second type of dream is more of a one-off encounter and can occur at any time during the grief process. The one who has died is sighted in good health and full of vigour, sometimes making contact with the dreamer, sometimes the dreamer glimpsing them at a distance. In some instances, the person may have been dead for some years and contacts a member of the family to look after another member.

I have also encountered two other types of dreams. Precognitive dreams occur as a series of dreams a few months prior to the death of someone close and alert the dreamer that the death is coming. The significance of such dreams only becomes apparent after the death has occurred. Debbie, the woman who created the garden after her father died, had the following dreams which, in hindsight, made sense of her father's death:

> First, I dreamed I went to the garage and drove out my mother's vintage car which hadn't been driven for forty years. (My parents had been married for forty years.) Then I dreamed of a pavilion in a park: the blinds were shut and it was a place of extreme calm and peace. Indeed it was a place of such deep peace that I knew it was where people go when they have just died and I was fearful I was seeing my own death, so I

didn't say anything to my partner, although I dreamed
of this place several times over the following weeks.
The final time the blinds were open. Six days later my
father died and it was then that I knew that what I had
been seeing was the place where he would go on his
death to heal. I was acutely aware of him in this place
and felt a strong connection with him there. Four days
after his death I started to lose him. The silver cord
had stretched and he was moving off with his mother
through some lawned gardens. It was dusk on the same
day I had seen ten days previously. Three weeks later to
the day I knew he had finally passed over, left the pavilion in the park and walked on — gone. The pavilion
was now shut up, closed, private. The work was done.

Katrina, whose father died when she was in Nepal, maintained contact with him through her dreams after he died
and it was he who told her of her mother's imminent death:

In the first dream my father described to me that he
was in a plane of existence wherein all the senses were
heightened. Everything looked and felt better there
and he had discovered that beer tasted especially good
in this place. He said that this plane existed parallel to
ours, it's just that we on the earth plane couldn't see
it. In the second dream, he was dressed in a formal
outfit, like one might wear in the 1920s, but somehow
updated. He told me that after a certain period, those
who die all receive an 'assignment' which is much like
a job or occupation. He had been assigned the task of
librarian in this big cosmic library. People who have
died have access to this library and can take out the
books at their leisure. Apparently, these books contain

all the information known in the Universe. The last
dream I had was when he told me he was waiting for
my mother and she died about two weeks later. I never
had these sorts of dreams about my mother, nor any
other dreams (of this nature) of my father since. However, when I sold my parents' house after my mother's
death, something extraordinary occurred. My mother
loved butterflies and collected images of them. On
the day I moved everything out of the house, I shifted
a dresser to the side and there on the floor was a tiny
passport picture of my father. Then out of nowhere
this beautiful butterfly, a variety that I have never seen
here before or since, flew in through the window and
alighted on the picture of my father. That was the very
last 'message' I had from either of them. I think that
once my father died, they both moved on to wherever
it is they needed to go.

The 'extraordinary' dream, if it occurs, appears to do so
approximately three-to-six months after the loved one dies
and is a final encounter in the grief season which leaves the
dreamer in a state of euphoria. This was Debbie's experience
two and a half months after her father died:

I dream of a young, handsome man who tells me he
is leaving for Finland and that he has come to say
goodbye. Between us there is a profound love that isn't
sexual, an amazingly deep bond. He tells me he will
send me letters from time to time, but they will be
anonymous and then he leaves and I realise this is my
father and now he is leaving for 'Fin' ('fin' means 'the
end' in French) land. I wake intensely and emotionally
moved.

Ellen had this dream three months after her father died:

> I am with a friend I have known forever, a good child-
> hood friend called Michael. We are in a gathering.
> There is a large crowd. Michael is singing a song to the
> tune of 'Don't forget to remember me, my love'. He
> is young, athletic, healthy, full of vigorous energy and
> has short, black, wavy hair. My relationship with him
> is extremely comfortable. Good friends. Non-sexual.
> As I watch him singing, his eye catches mine and I
> suddenly feel this enormous and powerful pain in my
> heart chakra as we recognise each other. It is a deep
> connection. This energy is so powerful it wakes me
> up. It has literally taken my breath away and I think it
> has been a dream about my animus. Then I realise this
> was the man I had known as my father in this life and
> would know again as 'Michael' in a future life when
> we met. I've often wondered how it is that you can be
> introduced to someone and have the sense of 'know-
> ing' them instantly, even though you've only just met
> for the first time.
>
> I had it when I met my partner, an instant 'know-
> ing' and recognition of each other. Of course the
> human part takes longer to understand what is hap-
> pening, but it suddenly made sense of my dream and I
> found it comforting. It didn't deny the father-daughter
> relationship we had had in this life and it didn't stop
> the process of pain and grief. It simply made sense.

Grief tosses time like a salad, mixing memories from the
past with an echo-silent future. In the minute intervals,
in the intolerable moments and the elongation of years
that follow the death of someone close to us, the body and

the mind continue to use their own intelligences to sort through the ideas, feelings and experiences of a lifetime of relationship. Some of these feelings may have lain dormant for many years, unconsciously hidden on the seabed of existence and only now exposed by the death. Others may involve the shocking recognition that words said in haste can now never be unsaid. In whatever way it occurs, if you are attending to the pain of grief and doing all that you can to acknowledge and give voice to your feelings in a way that brings completion, then you will heal on the far side of time.

Where grief can't flow — a sea with no tides

Society conditions us to avoid grief, since the outward expression of it can make other people feel helpless and uncomfortable. How often do we hear of people in loss described as 'putting on a brave face to the world'? We want the person in grief to change their behaviour so we can feel better, so we use intellect to couch the discomfort. Physiotherapist Sarah Key, interviewed by Margaret Throsby on ABC Radio Classic FM, Australia, 7 February, 2000, talked of 'people's zippered mouths' when they didn't want to discuss her son's cot death at the age of ten-weeks. Parents of a stillborn child are advised to 'have another baby'. Parents of a young child who has died are told they are 'still young enough to have another child'. Widows or widowers are told they can remarry. Such advice, whilst intellectually correct, is insulting and emotionally unproductive, for it ignores the emotional pain and does not offer a pathway for dealing with these feelings. This stems from an incorrect understanding of grief, underpinned by Replacement Theory.

What a person in grief wants most of all is to be heard without judgment and discrimination. What they need and what people tell them are in conflict, resulting in feelings of confusion, frustration and being double bound. When we are socialised not to express what we feel, we are led to emotional isolation. When we are expected to join in activities as usual without acknowledging the intensity of the loss, we are led to physical isolation. We can't grieve alone, yet as a society we physically isolate those in grief because we can't handle their despair. Ignoring a category of people in society does not make them go away, and treating grief as invisible merely pushes it underground. As has already been noted, normal and natural feelings of loss include shock and numbness, bodily distress, anger, idealization, guilt, hostility, replacement and panic. Grief reactions that are stuck in a loop going nowhere, on the other hand, mean constant bodily distress, endless anger, constant idealization, continuous guilt, extended hostility, persistent panic, substantial emotional and physical isolation and the unending need to replace the dead with another baby/husband/wife/mother/father, and so on. What someone in grief needs replaced is not the person who has died, but some of the things that person may have contributed to the relationship had they lived, such as love, friendship, physical touch, emotional support, listening, and acceptance. If the expression of grief is choked in this way, the natural healing chemicals produced by the body become choked along with it. The immune system remains dysfunctional and is more likely to produce illness and disease. If grief continues to be suppressed, these illnesses can turn into more serious conditions such as rheumatoid arthritis, ulcerous colitis, asthma, anorexia nervosa and neuro-dermatitis. All of these can be chronic, incapacitating and sometimes fatal.

Research has found that mortality rates are roughly the same for widowed women as for married women, yet are considerably higher for widowed men than for married men.[34] Furthermore, it has established that widows with acquaintances who made it easy for them to cry and express their intense feelings were healthier than those who experienced less encouragement from others to weep and discuss their feelings of grief.[35] It has also revealed that more men than women die following a distressing major life event and that men died at an earlier age.[36]

When your body remembers

In his book, *Swann's Way*, Marcel Proust experienced an 'all-powerful joy' as he dipped a Madeleine (a small cake) into his hot tea. Initially confused by such intense recall, he then remembered how, as a young boy, his aunt had showered him with Madeleines and this had become anchored to the memory.[37] Most of us have had similar experiences to this. Caught in the midst of the now, a particular aroma, flavour, vision, sound or even a movement can obliterate the moment and plunge us instead into three-dimensional sensations from yesteryear. Why is this so?

Sad, happy, traumatic or exultant experiences — and the whole range of qualities in between — shape our sense of who we are, what we do, and how we do it, on a moment to moment basis. These experiences are retained in the body and become part of the body's matrix of ongoing survival. If we have undergone traumatic experiences, they produce stress and suffering. It has long been recognized by alternative practitioners that stress can be released physically from the body through acupuncture, Rolfing, therapeutic touch, Reiki, polarity therapy, and chiropractic work. Whilst working physically on the body, practitioners often describe clients having a similar experience to Marcel Proust, a phenomenon known as somatic recall, the recall of memories of events that are stored in or accessed by the soft tissues of the body. Hence touching someone can release memory traces and even communicate them to another person. Physiologist J.Z. Young went further and suggested that the ways the body had been used or misused were incorporated into the structure of connective tissue. The organisms of the body then made predictions or 'forecasts' that promoted future survival.[38] Biophysicists exploring the scientific basis for these complementary healing methods and alternative medicines, suggested that connective tissue structure contained the history of what the organism had undergone in its existence. These were genetic, indicating ancestral physical survival techniques, and acquired, detailing the preferences, routines and adversities we had each undergone in our lifetime. Collagen fibres oriented themselves on the assumption that we would continue following the same patterns.[39] Body memory thus takes the qualities of the experiences of past events which have become incorporated into the soft tissues of the anatomy, files them away and then under appropriate circumstances, makes predictions for the future and holds onto these predictions as a survival mechanism until provided with a new pattern. If these 'memories' are released and their direction reoriented through the help of alternative therapies, the body can build newer and more successful pathways for sustaining bodily and emotional health. If trauma remains locked into body memory, it causes disease.

Personal time and cyclic memory

Whilst physical recall is triggered by the senses, emotional recall is triggered by time. 'Personal time' can be defined as the time which belongs to the landscape we shape by the things we do in that time. If we have encountered anxious, upsetting or painful events, then those memories will be recalled when time meets that same date again in a future cycle. Some of the reminders are full of warmth and love. A young man sent the following email to A Word A Day, an online service which posts a vocabulary term and its definition to thousands of subscribers every day:

> **Word: Avid**
>
> Quick note to say how much I enjoy AWAD. My brother David set me up with a gift subscription about a year or so ago. He died of cancer six months ago, so in an odd sort of way I'm still getting emails from him. Better still, on his birthday, 16 October, the word of the day was 'avid' — four letters from his name![40]

As a society, dates hold particular significance in our memory. Anzac Day (25 April) in Australia, Remembrance Day (11 November) in England, Australia and the USA (where it is called Veterans' Day), and Holocaust Remembrance Day or Yom Hashoah, (27 Nisan in the Hebrew calendar which corresponds to April-May in the Gregorian or civil calendar) are a few examples of society's need to remember and venerate the past. We do the same on a personal level and whilst some dates are overt, like the anniversary of a death, many dates are unconscious until events remind us of similar instances that occurred during the previous cycle of time. For whilst science would entice us into believing that time is linear, the foundations for how we understand time are, first, the rotation of the earth on its own axis which gives us the day, and secondly, the orbit of the earth around the sun which gives us the period of a year. This cyclic nature of the universe is the fundamental organ through which humanity operates. As Bernadette Brady says:

> We are led to believe in our busy, self-absorbing world that time is linear, that it comes to us but once and once passed, is lost forever.
>
> This may be true biologically in terms of your age and body, but it is not true in terms of how you experience the world. Time is not based on a linear concept, visiting but once like a finite piece of string stretching off into the distance. Rather it is circular, a loop, and consequently visits again and again and again. You do get a second chance with time and events, sometimes even a third and fourth chance.[41]

If every Monday you do a particular task, it is easy for you to base your internal clock on this regular repetitive event. As human beings we respond to rhythms and cycles, from the beat of our heart to the rising and the setting of the sun. This has its counterpart in cyclic memory. Time, returning to a point where a distressing event has occurred and which has been anchored in some way by the body's reactions, will inundate the body with that emotional and sometimes physical memory. Thus time is a shaped terrain of unconscious impressions, remembrances and learned responses to which we return cyclically and react accordingly and grief becomes a landscape through which we walk in time. We can chart that landscape as follows:

'The dangerous and death-bearing day'[42]

News of the death, however it arrives, binds with the emotions and locks itself into body and emotional memory. Whether the result of a long illness or a sudden and unexpected death, the date, place and corresponding gut feelings containing both shock and disbelief, are caught in the net of time and anchored as a significant event for the rest of the person's life. We see this most clearly with the death of public figures and major events of great note. People remember where they were and how they were feeling when they heard the news of JFK's assassination, or learnt of the death of Princess Diana, or when they saw the Twin Towers fall on 9/11.

If, however, you are lucky enough to be with your loved one when they die, whether at home, in hospital or in residential care, and to stay with them for an elongated amount of time afterwards, you will be gifted with an opportunity and a life-changing phenomenon precious beyond measure and profound in its illumination, for this is a time where death and love can meet. Hearing is the last sense to go as we die. My mother told me how she held my father's hand through the long night as he lay in a coma, dying. She told him that she loved him and he squeezed her hand. My aunt, sitting with her, noticed the green lines on the oscilloscope flatten and as they continued to sit with him, they saw his face change. Even though the body cools and the skin colour pales, the face takes on a radiance and beauty all of its own. There is a feeling of completion and wholeness, and an understanding of this exchange of life for death that is beyond reason and logic. Indeed, by placing one's hand lightly on the crown of the person's head, it is even possible, though not always, to feel the life force for some hours afterwards streaming out as it leaves the body. Attending the body in this way gives us an understanding of the process of death that is rare in modern society. Stephen Levine noted how 'To be able to be around the body of one who has just died for four or five or eight hours afterwards allows an understanding of the process of death unparalleled in our experience.'[43] Isabel Allende called this 'midwifing a person into death', in the same way as we midwife an incoming soul into birth. For those who have experienced this, it becomes clear that death is not the end of life. It is a time when whatever we term the essence of the beloved ceases to inhabit the body.

The funeral

The funeral is a public statement of changes that have occurred within the larger community. Whatever role our beloved has played in society, whatever their age, a shift occurs and that shift needs to be acknowledged and the roles adjusted. Funerals are the time when we pay our last respects to the one who has died and dispose of the body in a manner that reflects their life. It is when we become aware of the finiteness of time and the fragility of life. Above all, it is where we make the first public statement about this deep loss. Whilst funerals contain the rites and rituals society or religion demand for the appropriate disposal of the dead, funerals are not for the dead but for the living, the ones who are left behind. Funerals facilitate the healing process by being meaningful to the person in grief. They serve to bring together friends and relatives to share in the experience and to re-establish a network of support through the time ahead. Accepting help and support from others is essential at this time, for it is difficult to move through grief alone. The funeral is both a personal reminder and an outward signal that the one in grief is beginning a process of inward reflection. Since our senses connect emotions to events, the music one chooses for the funeral and the clothes one wears become anchors which flood the memory with recall. One interviewee told me: 'We chose a piece of music for my father-in-law's funeral and for years I could never listen to it again because it had been anchored to his death.' Clothes worn at the funeral often never get worn again, for the same reason.

One week later

The history of the week is uncertain. Once established, however, there is no record of the seven-day week ever being broken. Today it is enforced by global business, banking and the media, particularly television. A week, like a carousel, is a contained unit. Generally we know the form of what we will be doing on each day of the week, not necessarily the content. As a result, many people describe sunset on the day one week later as the time when they feel at their worst. The day and the time set off an explosion of emotional memory connected with the death, a cloudburst of 'memory pain' which is intense and emotional.

Four-to-six weeks later

Four-to-six weeks later the body's protective devices start to wear off, revealing the depth of the pain, the loneliness, and the intense sadness. By now society expects a person to have 'got over' their grief and supportive people are usually physically no longer around to help. Friends and relatives will do many practical and caring actions in the short term, but at such a critical point, when a person needs to talk about their feelings, their confusion and how upset they are over and over again and to be heard without judgement, people around them are less tolerant of any demonstration of sorrow and anguish. As a result, people often feel like they are getting worse, not better.

The prelude to the anniversary

At around eleven months after the death, people in grief describe being flooded by the same feelings and reactions they experienced immediately following the death. This prelude to the anniversary of the death activates the body's emotional memory and can manifest as minor or even major infections.

The anniversary of the death

Overall, the first year is painful and intense and its turning signifies a huge milestone, for time has now placed its hands around all the important shared dates: birthdays, anniversaries, Christmas Day, and so on. Now the spaces between the pain grow longer and often it is in this second year that one gains the full impact of the realisation that time has stopped forever for the one who has died. From now on 'anniversary reactions' will inundate a person in grief with reminders of the one who has died. This often means painful memories and the grief can return with a deluge of sensations as full as their initial impact. Anna had this experience:

I saw my father for the last time in September 1993, five months before he died. Just before my partner and I left the house he said, 'I want you to have the grand-mother clock', a request I had apparently made to him as a young girl. The grandmother clock had been in our family for several generations. It wasn't valuable. I just loved it. And then he continued, quite out of the blue, 'Don't forget us!' meaning both my parents, something he had never said before to me. When he died there was a dispute over who should get the clock. My mother wanted it to go to my brother, the eldest son, since he was the one who, at that time, had chil-dren. However, since my father had made this state-ment in front of my partner, my mother grudgingly agreed that I was now the rightful owner. Since I lived in Sydney and my mother lived in Brisbane, it had to be carefully packed and shipped. The clock arrived at our house on the first anniversary of my father's death. That afternoon my partner and I were shopping in the supermarket. As I placed a tin of fruit into the trolley, I was galvanized to the spot. The song playing in the supermarket was Nat King Cole singing *Unforgettable*.

And then?

There is no hard and fast edge to this chronology. The forever-ness of the death becomes increasingly apparent around six weeks and the intense expression of sadness and despair is most acute in the first three months. The first year of bereavement is immensely painful. It may be intense for the whole year, yet there will also be periods between the peaks of pain when the person in grief can sustain themselves quite comfortably and even enjoy events. Anniversaries, Christmas, a birthday or a significant date in the calendar for the family may trigger the pain and this often carries through into the second year of loss. McKissock referred to a person in grief in the first two years following the death as 'the newly-bereaved'. Two years appears to be the minimum time that a person needs to come to terms with the loss of someone close to them and five years appears to be long enough to integrate this. Some people may take longer; some may take less. Any number of events can trigger memories, engulf the present and surprise us by the level of distress produced by small things. In that moment, the pitch and power of loss is as acute, present and at the same level of intensity as when the person died. The difference is that, as long as it is not suppressed, the inundating emotion does not last as long, nor does it incapacitate in the way it did in the first two years. Given that time is the medium grief uses to change chapters in a person's life, then five years is a short distance to travel in reorganising our life in a way that is as meaningful to us after the death as it was prior to it.

* * *

Encountering Proteus
The paradox of time without end and time passing

Time	Reaction	Feelings
ACUTE GRIEF: the initial response — THE FUNERAL / THE FIRST FEW WEEKS	Shock and disbelief. Fear. Reduced concentration: dazed, confused, preoccupied. Numbness — may last moments, hours, days, sometimes months. There is little pain at this point.	Tearful. Restless and agitated. Disrupted sleep and eating patterns. Physical responses such as backache, headache, chest pain, nausea, vomiting, diarrhoea, menstrual problems. Emotional highs and lows. Often wants company — not to talk — just to be there.
4-6 WEEKS	Pain. Intense sadness. General feelings of nervousness and excessive tiredness. Loneliness, isolation, and despair.	Increased crying. Need to talk about feelings over and over again. Bodily distress such as backache, headache, diarrhoea or constipation.
DISINTEGRATION: the period of disengagement from the world — THE FIRST 2 YEARS 'the newly-bereaved'	Belief and disbelief. Extreme yearning. If anger, it is often a reflection of no longer being able to repair the relationship with the one who has died and is frequently projected onto those around: God, doctor, family, friends, and even the dead person. Finality not yet real.	Overt grief. Preoccupation with the image of the deceased. May sometimes hear the voice or develop physical symptoms of the dead person. Dreams of the deceased are vivid and of a different quality from 'normal' dreams. This is not the time to make major decisions as the healing process is in action.
Can last from 2-5 years	Belief and disbelief continue. Sadness. Despair. Fact and permanence are now real. 'Anniversary reactions' — of the death, birthdays, Christmas Day, and important shared dates — trigger reminders of the deceased.	Disorganisation of life style. Preoccupation with memories. Grief comes in waves'.
REINTEGRATION back into the community in a new and productive role.	'Out-of-the-blue' return to feelings of sadness and despair.	Re-establishing previous relationships and activities in ways that are irrevocably changed. Developing new friendships. Initiating a lifestyle that has reinvigorated energy and strength.

© D. Gunzburg 2000

One Person's Pathway

Ewan's brother, Paul, died from cancer aged forty-one at Easter, 2000. Paul was sixteen months older than Ewan, and he described it as a close relationship in a close family. The following are some of Ewan's email correspondence with me following Paul's death. They are revealing in the range and intensity of his feelings and offer his unique perspective in the rainbow of options called grief in the first three years after the death of his brother:

Seven months after the death:
23 November, 2000

Back from the first big family occasion without Paul, an aunt and uncle's fiftieth wedding anniversary. My aunt had her own scrape with cancer several years ago, before Paul was ill, and we worried, of course. She's one of my favourite people but... I don't know quite how to say it... somehow it would have been easier to understand if it was her rather than Paul that had lost the battle. I hate saying something like that but it is true. The day was a bit of a struggle. I didn't deal with it too well, but my Dad opened up a little for the first time. We went through his diary of Paul's last few months. I'm intrigued and proud of the fact that Paul insisted on getting the bus in to hospital, rather than getting a lift, just nine days before he died. There are times when I wonder what more I could have done and then I am reminded what fierce independence we were dealing with. A year ago Paul had just spent a week in hospital, told a white lie to get out (that our younger brother would be at his flat to look after him) and then emailed us all with Martin Luther

King's *Free At Last* speech. And I've just remembered
this one. My younger brother was driving with Paul
through the Devon countryside one night a couple of
years ago when they saw a man with a scythe climb-
ing over a gate. 'Tell me,' says Paul, 'that you saw him
too.' I know I have to keep talking about Paul and
writing about him. I'm terrified of boring my friends,
although to be honest, they insist they understand. I
can't bottle it up. I have his face beaming down from
a photo among his music and his books and it takes
nothing to set me off. What I wish is that Paul had
been able to say to me that he didn't think he was going to survive. I would have done things differently.

27 November, 2000

I've been thinking hard about your question about
what I would have done differently. It even kept me
awake last night. About a year ago he and I went on
a train journey to the place where we grew up (and
left in 1973) and the only specific words I remember
from all our conversations that day were him saying,
'This isn't going to kill me.' I'm sure he was convinced
of that then. Five months later he was dead and
somewhere in between I think he changed his mind
but he never told me. His death shocked me because I
still believed him. I knew he was really ill but I didn't
think it was near the end. If I'd known, I would have
told one of his oldest friends, his best man, who hadn't
seen him for two years, to go and see him quickly.
He lives the other side of the country and has lots
of kids and money is tight, but he's been so upset at
not seeing Paul more recently, although they talked

on the phone. If I'd known, I would have spent a
pointless weekend with him in his flat. He loved his
independence, but he wouldn't have said no. I had
saved my holiday allocation from work for later in the
year in case he got ill and I needed to take time off,
but that seems silly now. I know that I had to devote
time to Rachel and Brenna (my wife and daughter)
too, but if you know someone's time really is so short,
it would be understandable to see him more. If I'd
known, I would have rung him every day, not once or
twice a week. The last time I saw him alive, two days
before he died, are two things that give me comfort.
We were talking, alone, and he talked about what he
wanted done with his ashes (we would talk about such
things occasionally). For a second I wanted to rush
to his side and grab him and tell him everything he
meant to me, how I couldn't imagine things without
him, no doubt getting highly emotional at the same
time. But I stopped myself and I'm glad because it
would have frightened the hell out of him (as well
as me) and made him think I thought the battle was
over. He knew how I loved him anyway and he was
so brave I just couldn't buckle then and I asked him if
talking about his ashes meant he was pessimistic and
he said: 'Hell no, I've just bought my season ticket for
Somerset Cricket Club!' We laughed and I felt better
and now I wish I'd said, 'But seriously Paul...' And,
secondly, when we said goodbye, Rachel, Brenna and I
were getting in the car and Paul wasn't with us because
he was so breathless he couldn't leave his flat and I
got this sudden urge to run back to him, which I did,
and I told him, as he lay on his new red sofa, that I

would be with him as much as he wanted me to be, that he had to be honest with me and ask me to come even if he didn't think I'd want to and he agreed and seemed touched and I went and that was the last time I saw him alive. If he'd told me then (and it would have been an ideal time), what could I have done? The next day I spent with his children and he went into hospital, and the following one we were about to leave to visit him in hospital when the call came that he'd died. Honestly I don't know what I would have done differently. (This email could have started with that sentence and saved us both a lot of time.) Thanks so much for writing. I can't tell you how you've helped.

Nine months after the death:
6 January, 2001

Rachel has been incredibly sick. She's eight weeks pregnant today. We've only told our families. We had a miscarriage before Brenna was born, so we're taking it cautiously. It has perked us all up a bit. 'It's brought us some sparkle back,' Dad said. I can't believe we're having a baby Paul never knew. I'm so happy about it, and Rachel, too, but I'm still mourning for Paul, so feel a bit mad, up and down, but some sense of renewal I can't really express. Odd. I was born sixteen months after Paul was born, and if all goes well this baby will be born sixteen months after Paul died. I had an email from a journalist friend at Christmas saying her youngest sister was knocked down and killed by a van in the city. She was buried on her twenty-first birthday. Odd (again) how dealing with other people's grief somehow helps us come to place our own. Paul came up in a conversation with a bloke at work the other day, someone I don't know that well, and he said, 'Do you miss him a lot?' That is the dream question for me. I could have kissed him. A hard question to ask, but the one I hope for. It's the people who have the courage to ask without thinking you're going to crumple in a heap on the floor, or not minding if you do. I've been going back over my time with Paul, looking at our relationship and crying like he died last week which is how it feels. I miss his wit. I miss his calls on Saturday morning with the kids. I miss his voice. I miss his enthusiasm. I miss his awkwardness. I miss the face he would make as he peeled oranges.

Ten months after the death:
7 February, 2001

Looking at my history with Paul has made me realise we were really OK with each other. We had always spoken honestly with each other. Did I tell you he wrote letters for us all for after he died? We had ups and downs but downs never lasted long. There's not an awful lot of baggage and I can say that honestly, having gone through things over and over. Maybe more will come up in time, but that's really how it is now. Step by step. 'You were brilliant Ewan. You played a blinder,' he wrote to me. Still wish I'd done more though. Rachel had her first scan today, and the baby is looking fit and well, which is a huge relief. Came out of the hospital and rang our families from the cafe nearby. Missed telling Paul terribly. He is so tied up with this new life, doesn't matter if it's a boy or girl, he/she will be forever linked with Paul.

18 February, 2001

Had my Dad on the phone last night. Somehow it opened it all up in me, immediately and deeply. All that new strength I felt was beginning to arrive has evaporated again. Missed Paul more last night than ever. Somehow. This grief thing is like nothing else, isn't it?? My birthday in a couple of weeks — when I reach forty-one, the same age he'll be for ever.

The anniversary of the death:
12 April 2001

We're down to see my parents this weekend, along with my younger brother and his family. Rather like last year in fact. Except, except. Something slipping over me about Paul. Can almost physically feel it. Thanks for helping me this last year.

Fourteen months after the death:
28 June 2001

A beer with one of my oldest mates who spoke at Paul's funeral. Talk about work and babies and house prices and, inevitably, Paul. Sets me crying. Met another old friend the other day whose son was killed in a fire at the age of twenty-four a couple of years ago. No body for her to look at, he had to be identified by DNA. Paul's life is rich and full compared to him and I realise how lucky we were to say goodbye to his lovely crumbling old body. She remembers practically nothing of her son and I remember practically nothing of Paul. Is this at all common? Is it a human reaction in helping us to cope, because if it is, I don't want it. I want more memories please.

Seventeen months after the death:
10 September, 2001

(In late August Rachel gave birth to a little girl, Celeste). If she had been a boy in some ways the connections to Paul may have even been too strong. I can sense the disappointment in some people's voices when they hear she is a girl, thinking perhaps that I wanted a boy. I didn't. I wanted a life, a new life that would breathe back happiness and renewal and corny-sounding stuff like that. When Rachel had gone with the nurse for a shower a few hours after the birth, I told Celeste all about her Uncle Paul and how I wish they could have met. I miss the enthusiasm and excitement he would have had at the news. On Thursday I will be exactly the age Paul was when he died. But he'll always be my big brother. Reading this I sound so glum but I'm fantastically happy about Celeste. Weird emotions.

Twenty months after the death:
3 December, 2001

George Harrison's death rather shook me. I'd say that it brought it all back about Paul's death, except it's never gone away. I knew Harrison was really ill, but you hope it's not that. I had an hour or so out of the office, but it was Paul that I was crying about, not Harrison.

Twenty-one months after the death:
4 January, 2002

I hate the speed of time. 2001 is the first full year Paul never knew. I now cannot say he died last year. I don't want the waters to close over him. I want everyone to be shocked still that he can be dead at forty-one. That's what I hate about a new year.

The second anniversary of the death:
9 April, 2002

I'm no monarchist, but seeing the faces of the royal
family at the funeral of the Queen Mother on the
news today brought it home how grief touches us
all. Nobody could have less in common than the
Queen Mother and Paul — nobody — it makes me
laugh thinking how on earth they could — but I was
changing 'she' and 'her' to 'he' and 'him' in the funeral
service and I liked what I heard.

Two years and three months after the death:
2 July, 2002

Just got through the second anniversary of scattering
Paul's ashes. Made me feel quite aware that I'm going
at a different speed to everyone else. I still want people
to be shocked, but realise that just saying 'two years
ago' makes it sound like an age.

Two years and eleven months after the death:
3 March, 2003

I got Tony Benn's latest diaries for Christmas.[44] His
wife died of cancer a few months after Paul in 2000.
Reading about it got to me. I wrote to him and had
a good card back the other day telling me about his
elder brother who died in WW2 aged twenty-two.
He says he still misses him, nearly sixty years later.
I realise I get some kind of comfort from writing to
people Paul knew or admired to get some reaction.
I still love telling people about him. The other day I
was assembling Paul's rambling old sound system that
I inherited and Brenna, who was 'helping', said, 'Do
you wish Uncle Paul was here to help us?' (because he
would have done it in two minutes) and I said I did

and she said, 'He would probably have forgotten how
to do it by now because he did die a long time ago.' To
her maybe.

The third year:
21 December 2003

I was talking to Brenna about my deputy editor who
recently gave birth to a dead nine-pound baby boy and
she said how sorry she was that she didn't meet him
before he died. I would sooner she and Celeste didn't
grow up afraid of talking about death, but it's hard
to know the right way to go about it. I congratulated
my deputy editor and her husband on their large col-
lection of Christmas cards, but she said most of them
were bereavement cards she hadn't taken down yet!

Into the future …

The future is a place which does not contain the beloved.
This painful and often shocking fact takes time to
comprehend. When we are used to our lives being witnessed
by those close to us, when the slow build of history and the
continuity of a life lived together ends, it seems impossible
for life to continue without our loved one. Death freezes
that relationship in the countryside of time. We can only
imagine the portrait time might have painted of their lives.
The reality is that now they never change, neither in looks
nor in temperament. Life no longer has any effect upon
them. They remain 'my older brother' or 'my father who
died when I was eleven' or 'my two-month old baby' no
matter what age we reach. What does happen, if they are
older than us, is that when we reach the age they were
when they died, we realise just how young they were and
how much more of life they could have had to live.

In 1973, when I was in my late teens and still living in Perth, Western Australia, my home town, I read an article published in *The West Australian* newspaper announcing the death of a poet at the age of twenty-four and lamenting the end of his promising career. The family had published a book of his poetry privately in remembrance. The book was entitled *Light Me A Candle* and the poet's name was Michael Dransfield. Profoundly moved by the poem, I memorised it:

> Tonight there's a mother whose child has died
> rocking herself to sleep,
> With her fingers curled for the touch of her son
> who lies in a bloodied heap.
> She does not dream of a brave young man
> with a rifle, a curse and a girl,
> She dreams of a shy and loving lad
> who lived and was her world.

For years I kept the newspaper clipping until finally it became lost in the caravan of my life. Now time has washed away the details, the name of the poem, and how and why he died. Nevertheless, in 2019 Michael would have been seventy-one years old. I can make that leap. Even knowing he died at twenty-four, I can imagine him a successful published poet in the prime of his life, earning respect and veneration. The family can't do this. Freeze-framed in memory, he stays twenty-four. The home movie ends halfway through the first reel.

Death shakes us to the core of our being and puts us into a unique place with the one who has died. If the work of grief has been accomplished, then life re-establishes itself in concert with a newly-formed relationship with the dead, not forgetting them, not immobilized by the loss, but embracing what has happened and moving on with life. It is an important step to reach. It means a person can start building a relationship with the beloved without expectation of their return.

Returning to the world

Grief is a powerful process which grips a person's life. It is painful and that is part of its unspoken contract with us. It lets us know that for a time, things have changed. Like a broken bone, grief must be properly set in order for it to heal and function with strength once more, so any action a person in acute grief takes to articulate the pain is healthy. Achilles' reaction when he heard the news of Patroclus' death was an expression of the intensity of the pain he was feeling on the inside. It was not a conscious decision on his part; it was helping him to survive. When someone yells, kicks, screams or howls, their behaviour is neither bizarre nor pathological, nor will they become violent, even though in Homer's work Antilochus held Achilles' hands 'for fear of him cutting his throat.' The person is simply doing what he or she needs to do in order to stay alive by expressing what they are experiencing and how they are feeling. However it is conveyed, people in grief are communicating their perception of reality. For them the pain is valid, physical, and needs to be communicated. If we stop a person from doing this, it bottles up. If we impose a feeling of guilt on them for acting in this way, we encourage this suppression. Blocking grief can throw the person into secondary symptoms, such as depression or weight gain. There is nothing we can say that will take away this pain, nor does it need to be taken away. The pain 'is'. Nevertheless, since we are unaccustomed to seeing the expression of grief in the community, because we placate it and hide it away, we are generally not aware of the intensity or duration of the pain involved unless we've experienced it ourselves.

Hamlet is the story of a man in grief for his murdered father. Through the journey of the play he is awakened to death and comes to realise that death makes life possible:

> Not a whit, we defy augury. There is a special
> providence in the fall of a sparrow. If it be now,
> 'tis not to come; if it be not to come it will be now;
> if it be not now, yet it will come. The readiness is all...[45]

Readiness allows us to fully participate in life and to wholly engage in the ritual of loss when it occurs. Further it allows us to return to a changed and different world, changed because we are changed, different because we are no longer responding in the way we did before the loss.

The process of grief takes time. Grief is the recognition of a deeply-felt loss, a necessary process for a person to go through in order to be able to collect the shards of life that fragmented with the death and to go on living fully again. The process of grief is one which heals and its expression should never be equated with weakness. It is a rite of passage.

Notes

1. N. T. Croally and Roy Hyde, *Classical Literature: An Introduction* (London: Routledge, 2011), p.26.
2 Homer, *The Odyssey*, trans. E. V. Rieu (Harmondsworth: Penguin Books, 1946), pp.337-38.
3. John W. James and Russell Friedman, *The Grief Recovery Handbook* (New York: Harper Collins, 1998), p.3.
4. Mal McKissock, interview by Norman Swan, 2001. http://www.abc.net.au/radionational/programs/healthreport/2002-01-14/3503226

5.   Population figure from the US Census Bureau: http://www.census.gov/popclock/ - accessed 15 March 2019.

6.   Population figure from Office for National Statistics, UK: https://www.ons.gov.uk/peoplepopulationandcommunity/populationandmigration/populationestimates/articles/overviewoftheukpopulation/november2018 accessed 15 March 2019.

7.   William Shakespeare. 'Troilus and Cressida' (3.3.163-169) in Stephen Greenblatt et al., eds., *The Norton Shakespeare* (New York: W.W. Norton & Company, Inc., 1997), p.1877.

8.   Will Aid at https://www.willaid.org.uk/latest-news/more-half-british-adults-are-following-arethas-footsteps-and-have-no-will-survey - accessed 15 March 2019.

9.   Peta Bee, 'Love Drug: Why Women Are Getting into Anabolic Steroids,' (London: *The Independent On Sunday*, 2 March 2003); Peter Walker, 'Spiralling Anabolic Steroid Use Leaves UK Facing Health Timebomb, Experts Warn,' (*The Guardian*, 19 June 2015).

10. http://www.grief-recovery.com/request_index.htm - accessed 13 February, 2003.

11. http://www.grief.net/Media/Wall_Street_Journal.htm - accessed 24 February, 2003.

12. Michael Leunig, *The Prayer Tree* (Melbourne: CollinsDove, 1991), second page of Introduction.

13. Maurice Lamm, *The Jewish Way in Death and Mourning* (New York: Jonathan David Publications, 1969), p.1.

14. Charlene Spretnak, *The Resurgence of the Real: Body, Nature, and Place in a Hypermodern World* (New York; London: Routledge, 1999), p.183.

15. Elisabeth Kübler-Ross and Mal Warshaw, *Working It Through* (N.Y.: Macmillan, 1982), p.134.

16. M. Mitchell Waldrop, *Complexity: The Emerging Science at the Edge of Order and Chaos* (New York: Simon & Schuster, 1993), p.295.

17. Waldrop, *Complexity*, pp.330-31.

18. Mircea Eliade, *The Sacred and the Profane: The Nature of Religion*, trans. Willard R. Trask (Orlando: Harcourt, Inc., 1957), pp.68-69.

19. Joseph Campbell, *The Hero with a Thousand Faces* (London: Paladin, 1988), p.391.
20. Robert A. Johnson, *Owning Your Own Shadow: Understanding the Dark Side of the Psyche* (HarperSanFrancisco, 1991), pp.98-99.
21. Johnson, *Owning Your Own Shadow*, p.107.
22. Mal McKissock, *Coping with Grief*, 4th ed. (Sydney: ABC Enterprises, 1985), p.14.
23. David D. Franks, 'The Neuroscience of Emotions,' in *Handbook of the Sociology of Emotions*, ed. Jan E. Stets and Jonathan H. Turner (New York: Springer, 2006).pp.47-49.
24. C. S. Lewis, *A Grief Observed* (New York: Bantam Books, 1963), p.8.
25. William H. Frey II and Muriel Langseth, *Crying: The Mystery of Tears* (Minneapolis, MN: Winston Press, 1985), p.16.
26. James Elkins, *Pictures and Tears: A History of People Who Have Cried in Front of Paintings* (New York: Routledge, 2001).
27. Frey II and Langseth, p.13.
28. Charles Dickens, *Oliver Twist* (London: Chapman & Hall Ltd, 1907), p.266.
29. Alfred, Lord Tennyson. *The Princess*, The Poetry Foundation https://www.poetryfoundation.org/poems-and-poets/ poems/detail/45379 - accessed 17 November 2016.
30. Henry Maudsley. *The Pathology of Mind: A Study of Its Distempers Deformities and Disorders*. London: Macmillan & Co, 1895, p.138.
31. Jeffrey A. Kottler, *The Language of Tears* (San Francisco: Jossey-Bass Publishers, 1996), p.37.
32. William C. Chittick and Jalāl al-Dīn Rūmī (Maulana), *The Sufi Path of Love: The Spiritual Teachings of Rumi*, Suny Series in Islamic Spirituality (Albany: State University of New York Press, 1983), p.282.
33. Susanne Iles, 'The Storied Garden: Planting the Seeds of Myth,' *Spirituality & Health* 5 (June 2002).
34. K. J. Helsing, M. Szklo, and G.W. Comstock, 'Factors Associated with Mortality after Widowhood,' *American Journal of Public Health* 71, no. 8 (1981): 802-809, p.802.

35.   David Maddison and Wendy L. Walker, 'Factors Affecting the Outcome of Conjugal Bereavement,' *The British Journal of Psychiatry* 113, no. 503 (1967): 1057-1067, p.1057.

36.   Clifton D. Bryant and Dennis L. Peck, *Encyclopedia of Death and the Human Experience*, vol. 1 (Los Angeles: SAGE, 2009), p.993.

37.   Marcel Proust. *Swann's Way*. Translated by C.K.Scott Moncreiff. À La Recherche Du Temps Perdu, 1913-1927 (In Search of Lost Time). Edited by William C. Carter Vol. 1, (New Haven and London: Yale University Press, 2013), pp.50-53.

38.   J. Z. Young, *The Life of Mammals: Their Anatomy and Physiology* (Oxford: Clarendon Press, 1957), p.65.

39.   James L. Oschman and Nora H. Oschman, 'Somatic Recall Part 1 - Soft Tissue Memory,' *Massage Therapy Journal* 34, no. 3 (1995).

40.   http://wordsmith.org/awad/awadmail.html

41.   Bernadette Brady, 'Cycles within Cycles' *Wellbeing Astrology Guide* 2002, p.5.

42.   Hermes Trismegistus, *Liber Hermetis*, ed. Robert Hand, trans. Robert Zoller (Salisbury, Queensland: Spica Publications, 1998), p.28.

43.   Stephen Levine, *Who Dies? An Investigation of Conscious Living and Conscious Dying* (New York: Anchor Press, 1982), p.220.

44.   Tony Benn. *Free at Last! Diaries 1991-2001*. Edited by Ruth Winstone London: Hutchinson, 2002. Member of Parliament for forty-seven years. The grandson, son and father of MPs, Benn is widely regarded as one of Britain's greatest living Parliamentarians. He served as a Labour Cabinet minister for Harold Wilson and then James Callaghan 1974-1979. The term 'Bennite' refers to someone who adheres to radical left-wing politics.

45.   William Shakespeare. 'Hamlet' (5.2.157-160) in Greenblatt et al., p.1751.

2

How Do We Learn to Grieve?

My soul is a broken field, plowed by pain.
- Sara Teasdale, poet (1884-1933)

Like Menelaus there are countless ways we can founder in the bay and they occur extremely early in our lives. On many levels in western society we are taught to focus only on the surface of life and not to explore the depths. Through the circumstances of loss we rapidly learn that other people cannot or do not want to handle strong emotions and across our life we build up unconscious responses about how to deal with them. Sadly, within a short time after a death, even though we may be feeling the exact opposite, we are socialised to respond to the question, 'How are you?' with the woefully inadequate term, 'Fine'.

'...Weep and you weep alone'

Grief is an experience with which we have been struggling for thousands of years. Throughout history the catharsis of crying has consistently been articulated in poetry and literature. Two thousand years ago, Horace, the son of a freed slave in Rome who became one of the nation's greatest poets, gave voice to this feeling:

As man laughs with those who laugh,
So he weeps with those that weep;
If thou wish me to weep,

Thou must first shed tears thyself;
Then thy sorrows will touch me.'

Ars Poetica (V. 102)[1]

Ovid, the son of an old land-owning family of equestrian rank and one of the most prolific poets of Rome's Golden Age, observed:

It is some relief to weep; grief is satisfied and carried off by tears.

Tristium (IV. 3. 37)

And later:

Suppressed grief suffocates, it rages within the breast, and is forced to multiply its strength.

Tristium (V. 1. 63)[2]

Ovid's influence was felt from the Middle Ages to the Renaissance and his works shaped such Italian poets as Ludovico Ariosto and Giovanni Boccaccio and such English poets as Geoffrey Chaucer, John Gower, Edmund Spenser, William Shakespeare and John Milton. Egeon in Shakespeare's *The Comedy of Errors* declared:

O, grief hath changed me since you saw me last,
And careful hours, with Time's deformed hand,
Have written strange defeatures in my face.[3]

Proverbs handed down from generation to generation resonate with the benefits of psychogenic tears:

'Learn weeping and thou shall gain laughing.'
(*German*)
'Tears soothe suffering eyes.'
(*Persian*)

'What soap is for the body, tears are for the soul.'
(*Jewish*)
'He that conceals his grief finds no remedy for it.'
(*Turkish*)

Yet how often did our parents tell us: 'There, there, don't cry, it's alright.' 'You stop your crying or I'll give you something to cry about.' 'Please stop that crying, you're making your mother feel bad/upset/giving her a headache.' Such unsupportive reactions manipulate a child into believing that crying is a sign of weakness, vulnerability and immaturity.

One way behaviour gets lodged into the culture is through popular song. An example of this is *Crying in the Rain*, whose words and music were written by Howard Greenfield and Carole King. The lyrics are the battle cry of someone wounded by love who refuses to let anyone see them shedding tears. Even though their heart is broken, they have been taught that it is brave and courageous to hide their feelings, so using pride as a shield, they'll do their crying in the rain. We can perhaps trace this attitude back to the latter part of the nineteenth century, when American poet, journalist and free thinker, Ella Wheeler Wilcox gained extensive popularity with her nearly forty volumes of verse.[4] Although never regarded as a major poet, her audience was the readership of women's and literary magazines from which she earned herself a living, a rare feat for women of her day. By 1919 she was sufficiently well-known to be included in *Bartlett's Famous Quotations*. Her poetry was simple and mixed platitudes with sentimentality and though literary critics failed to be impressed, her messages of hope and comfort touched the hearts of readers of all ages and classes. Although her name may not be well-known, one of her lines of verse from a poem called *Solitude* is now common parlance when it comes to grief:

> Laugh, and the world laughs with you;
> Weep, and you weep alone.

First published in *The Sun*, 1883, when Wilcox was thirty-two years old, thence in *Poems of Passion* and in other newspapers in the years following, her poem continues:

> For the sad old earth must borrow its mirth,
> But has trouble enough of its own…

> Rejoice, and men will seek you;
> Grieve, and they turn and go.
> They want full measure of all your pleasure,
> But they do not need your woe.
> Be glad, and your friends are many;
> Be sad, and you lose them all.
> There are none to decline your nectared wine,
> But alone you must drink life's gall.[5]

Wilcox had a mass following amongst the non-literary at a time when newspapers and popular magazines regularly published verse for the unsophisticated. She encouraged these people to struggle through dull, unrewarding lives for the greater good of what they could achieve on a divine level. A sizeable audience sought comfort and wisdom from her words, so when this widely-read and well-received poem disseminated the idea that solitude and isolation were the appropriate solvents for the pain of grief, crying and grieving openly became unwelcome traits to cultivate, a social bias that has continued to this day.

Some years ago I was watching our (then) three-month old kitten carefully observing our older, head cat of some fifteen years. The older cat, who had a skin allergy around her mouth, was scrubbing her face vigorously with her paw after eating to alleviate the itch. Being young and impressionable, the small kitten also began to scrub his face, believing this was the way to wash on completion of a meal. After two or three scrubs he stopped. This action hurt his face and was uncomfortable on his whiskers. Not long afterwards I saw him wash his face with the soft, gentle action he maintained for the rest of his life. He had learned that if putting a deed into action hurt, he must change the action. Like other animals, we, too, copy the behaviour of our elders when we are young and looking for models by which to live. Considering our greater brainpower, it seems much harder for us to stop a learned behaviour when it hurts us. It takes an effort of will to consciously change a pattern of behaviour. Often it is painful to do so, yet in the long run it is worth it, for the consequences of that change can free us from the past.

Avert-and-Smother

Misconceptions our parents, unconsciously and with deep care, teach us about loss and which become enmeshed into the matrix come in this form: 'Don't feel bad, have a lolly.' 'Don't cry, we'll get you another... (animal).' 'Don't worry, there are plenty more fish in the sea.' On the surface these statements tell us to divert the pain by focusing attention elsewhere and then use a substance or an object to bury the problem. There are, however, unspoken commands embedded in communications such as these. Think back to a time when someone told you not to look at someone:

your immediate reaction was to look at them. In order not to do something, a person has to know what it is they are not supposed to do. Thus in telling someone not to do an action, they will automatically access the opposite command. An instruction like 'don't feel bad' is, on first impact, received as an injunction to feel bad, 'don't worry' is an embedded command to worry, and so on. Such double-messaging results in a confused response. Our reaction is to reach for a short-term solution designed to cover up or overarch the problem: Eat Something. Buy Something. Replace It With Something. As noted previously, food, alcohol, prescription drugs, illicit drugs or narcotics, a shopping expedition (ironically termed 'retail therapy'), one's work, one's anger or simply becoming lost in fantasy and illusion are amongst western society's temporary palliatives. Such words dismiss the value of the relationship and do nothing to complete the emotional pain caused by the loss. It also sets up a lifetime belief that feelings can be fixed by short-term solutions. Our focus may have been distracted, but such analgesics are not an answer. The loss and the network of feelings welded to the pain are simply smothered and entombed. We subscribe to the illusion that immediate relief from pain gives long-term ease. If we continue to use the Avert and Smother method with successive losses, life begins to implode. If we are unwilling to face the grief, it festers.

'What do I say?'

A person in grief needs to be acknowledged, not silenced. Yet people are often immobilized with awkwardness when they hear news of a death. They have been taught that saying something totally inappropriate is better than saying nothing at all, so they offer the trite and the banal: 'There are so many people worse off than you.' 'You'll find each day will be a little easier.' 'So how are you managing without a husband?' 'Separation is much more painful than bereavement.' Instead what the person in grief hears is a tactless comment coming from someone completely unqualified telling them how they should be feeling right now. Ill-chosen words reduce the internal experience and stop communication. Worse still is when what is offered is a hackneyed and worn-out cliché, a truth that began life as authentic but which has long since outworn its welcome. Often used as plug and play features in articles, they become inserted without thought as to their truth or appropriateness and sustained without the rigour of critical assessment. Glibness is excruciating. It indicates how little the person understands what they are saying and further, that they have never allowed themselves to tackle the desolation of loss and to be truly insightful about it. In Series Three, Episode Four of the American television series *The West Wing*, President Jed Bartlett (Martin Sheen) is given the task of informing the parents of two Americans that their sons, aged nineteen and twenty-one, have been the deliberate targets of a suicide bomber in Israel. Uncertain as to what to say, he runs through possibilities: 'My wife and I were terribly sorry to hear of the - ...', 'Please accept our deepest condolences on the occasion of - ...' Finally he lifts the receiver to his ear: 'Mr and Mrs Levy? This is President Jed Bartlett. I have three daughters. I have no idea what to say.'[6] Rather than cluttering the airwaves with unspoken fears, such communication opens a door to allow the other party to speak. People in grief need to ventilate what is happening on the inside of their reality without censure and without trepidation about the other person's reactions.

'I know how you feel!'

If you want to shrink the experience of the person in grief and deny the immediacy of the pain, tell them you know how they feel. If you want to kidnap the personal encounter of another as they confront loss or trivialise the unrepeatable and exclusive experience of their suffering, tell them you know how they feel. As each relationship is distinctively different, so no two losses are the same. The only common reality grief shares with each of us is the encounter with Proteus and any of the accompanying grass roots responses outlined in Chapter One. How each person engages with Proteus is their personal journey. Someone profoundly affected by grief can't distinguish between 'want' and 'able'. They feel a raw 'wanting' for someone to fill the yawning gap carved out by the death and in that state are highly vulnerable. A person in grief needs someone who can provide a supportive framework in which to feel safe. It takes courage to realise that it is impossible to guess at the pain of another in grief, nor even to begin to imagine how they must be feeling. All we can do is remember a time when loss tore us to the quick and the desolation and heartache that stayed with us for months and sometimes years was almost unbearable. The word empathy comes from the Greek 'empatheia' (from 'em-' meaning in and 'pathos' meaning feeling) and means the ability to understand and share the feelings of another, to be 'in-feeling' with them. It was first used in the 1920s by American psychologist E.B. Titchner when observing one-year olds imitating the distress of another person. Empathy focuses the listener's attention on the inner feelings of the other and asks that they spend more time listening and less time talking. When you tell someone that you know how they feel, you indicate that you are about to replace their experience with yours, that the urgency of their pain and their need to put this into words are being hijacked by someone with little feeling for their circumstances. Acknowledging that the person in grief needs to express their pain may well trigger grief that is still unresolved within us. It takes boldness and daring to be with a person in the fullness of their grief, neither condemning nor condoning, neither afraid of their loss nor the fears inside us, accepting and observing, listening and loving.

Comparison

Every loss is felt emotionally as a major loss. Author and humourist Mark Twain observed, 'Nothing that grieves us can be called little: by the eternal laws of proportion a child's loss of a doll and a king's loss of a crown are events of the same size.'[7] Comparisons such as 'Be glad you already have two other children' or 'Be glad you are still young enough to have another baby' are odious. They fail to recognise that intense feelings need to be dealt with the moment they happen in order to facilitate healing. Furthermore, whilst the length of time required to complete any unfinished business may differ, it is the quality of the relationship and the deeply-felt separation that causes pain. The loss of an animal friend may be just as intense and painful as the loss of a human relationship. It depends on the age at which the loss occurs and the nature of that relationship.

'You never get over the death of someone close to you.'
This belief is so ubiquitous one has to wonder about the
nature of the secondary gain in saying this. Here's how it
seems to work: the initial pain of the loss becomes anchored
to the memory of the person who has died. Believing life
is linear, we then, incorrectly, assume that if we stop the
pain, we stop remembering. The fear is that if we bound
back into our lives with our grief complete, we will lose
the memory of the person forever, so we come to define
ourselves by the pain of the loss and not by the memory of
our relationship to the person. To add to the complexity, if
the death has been the result of an accident or a long-term
illness which has ravaged the body, many people remember
the person they loved only in these final, difficult moments,
freeze-framing their life on this image and running that
loop time and time again, despite the fact that the many
years prior to this have been happy and joyful ones.

Here are two examples: Jane, in her mid-thirties, had
lived in Birmingham, England, all her life and came from
an extremely close family on her mother's side. Her Aunt
Deirdre, her mother's sister, met Uncle Andrew when they
were at high school in the 1940s. They were married after
the Second World War and stayed happily married. Early
in 2000, at the age of seventy-two, her Uncle Andrew
died suddenly from a massive heart attack, the first of her
mother's generation to die. 'Aunt Deirdre has been in an
awful state ever since,' said Jane. 'Not so long ago she broke
down on the phone to my mother, confessing she still can't
sleep because she keeps seeing Uncle Andrew collapsing in
the doorway over and over again.' When Jack (see Chapter
Four), in his forties, offered to go with his ex-wife to the

cemetery to visit their son's grave seven years after his death from a brain tumour, his wife replied that she appreciated his gesture but, unlike him, she had never been able to have any happy dreams or thoughts of their son. They were always nightmares. Her memory could only extend back to the last weeks, the horror of how he looked and the last moments of him dying. Her embedded memory was the result of strong emotions caused by major and profound loss, but the way the behaviour had been managed was inappropriate, for such memories were heavy burdens for her to carry for the rest of her life. Inside us we carry many images of our loved ones in all their life expressions. Debbie, whose father died unexpectedly at the age of seventy, wrote this three weeks after his death:

> He was a King Lear
> An ancient Celtic King
> Who filled everybody's lives
> With tears and with joy,
> With sadness and happiness
> And anger and peace.
> In short, he was a total father.

Resolution does not mean forgetting. Through the work of grief what we are resolving and completing is our relationship to the pain caused by the loss. As James and Friedman noted, pain does not equal love, love equals love.[8]

Time and the work of grief
One of the most misunderstood clichés is that 'time heals all wounds'. In a radio interview, Gretel Killeen, an Australian media personality, presenter, comedian, journalist and author, told of a key moment in her life

when she was twenty years old.[9] She and her boyfriend of four months were returning from the snowfields when they had a car accident. He died. She did not. 'I didn't know how much that changed me,' she said. 'I felt his parents had the right to grieve and I didn't want to swan in and take the stage.' So she buried her grief. Her next comment was revealing. She said that the common notion that time heals all wounds was incorrect. 'Time,' she said, 'makes you realise you'll never find anyone else like that.' Time itself does not heal anything, for time is not an actor on the stage of life. Time is the medium through which we move and it dulls our memory the further we slide away from the event, adding a coat of dust on all the unspoken, uncompleted things we needed to say, clogging, debilitating and finally choking our behaviour. We ourselves have to initiate and take action within a time frame in order for completion to occur. The action we take is the clutch plate between how things were and the way they can become. The work of grief is an active process, not a passive one, yet it requires nothing more than paying attention to the natural process that occurs inside a person when someone we love dies. This process begins with our memories.

Memory, the natural process
Memory is the ability to retain an impression of past experiences. We build up memories of someone close to us through a life-long process which combines continuity and change through daily interactions. Over time the relationship embraces the whole ocean of gestures, signals, fine distinctions, subtle shadings, and individual idiosyncrasies of everyday living which Celia J. Orona observed, 'tell me the other is who I perceive him/her to

be, and which in turn, lets me know he/she recognizes me.'[10] Relationships occur in absolute, clock time and are calendar-specific in how they begin (the first meeting, the birth of a child) and in how they continue (anniversaries and celebrations, as well as routines such as dental check-ups or weekly coffee meetings, and so on). The paradox is that whilst the narrative of the relationship is expressed through the passing of objective time, the relationship is experienced and undergoes change in subjective, lived time through created moments which have significance and value and in which both parties of the relationship place meaning. Memories, good and bad, sad and happy, excruciating and exhilarating, are socially constructed within the context of the two interwoven lives. The relationship also anticipates a future in which events will occur and are part of the unspoken agreement between the two people. This knowledge and identity of the other is processed into long-term memory through encoded information, but memories will always flush from the brain unless some process attracts them to stay. Sleep is the mechanism that appears to strengthen and integrate what we have learnt into our system.[11]

In the days, weeks, months, and years of a relationship, we not only witness the continuing identity changes of each other through the social construction of memory, but consolidate these changes through sleep and build thousands of minutes of memories. When someone we love dies, this natural and ongoing process stops and another natural process takes its place called the Grief Review, similar to the Life Review.

Life Review

In 1955 Robert N. Butler undertook the first long-term studies of healthy, older people aged sixty-five and above.[12] Similar studies were conducted at the same time at Duke University, Durham, North Carolina, USA. Both found identical results, that healthy older people in the community were mentally alert and active. As his studies progressed, Butler found a fascinating secondary phenomenon.[13] He noticed that the imaginative faculty and memories of the past of these older people contained great power and luminosity and that their ability to recall early parts of their life, both events and people, which may long since have been sorted and filed, could come flooding back into the present with crystal clarity. When it did, there was a desire to complete the memory, rather like completing a jigsaw. Indeed, the primary concern of this profound internal process appeared to be the desire to re-examine events in order to come to terms with what had happened in the past. Butler called this the Life Review and concluded that this was a normal function of later years. Using memories, reminiscence, and nostalgia, it was neither the pathological condition of someone living in the past, nor the confusions of a wandering mind. Instead it was an important psychological task of making sense of the life a person had lived as it neared its end. The life review could occur under peaceful conditions, remembering events with pleasure or communicating through storytelling, or it could contain regret, homesickness, and sentimentality.

The aims of the life review are to smooth out past differences, to compensate and make amends for lost opportunities, and to bring an end to hostilities with family members and friends, often after years of lost time. It is designed to heal psychic pain through putting one's life in order and in so doing, take the necessary steps towards death by reducing any anger, fear or apprehension. It might be told to passers-by, door to door salesmen, people in the street or to anyone who would pay attention or it could take the form of a personal interior monologue made audible to no-one's ears but the person's own. Life reviews could be convoluted, contain discrepancies and fallacies and were frequently filled as much with bitterness as with humour.

It is most striking in old age and in recent years a variety of psychotherapeutic techniques have been developed using this natural process, including structured life review therapy and guided autobiography.[14] As well, a number of life review and family history training manuals have been developed to guide older people on their journey. In Great Britain, Pam Schweitzer MBE formed Age Exchange, based in south-east London, in 1983 as a way of valuing reminiscence in the lives of older healthy people who were often lonely, as well as those in care environments. Through its outreach services Age Exchange offers Reminiscence Arts, the creative exploration of memories through workshops for community groups, and in educational and care settings. These often evolve into the creation of a piece of art, shared within a wider community setting or kept contained and personal.[15] Age Exchange recognised that the memories of ordinary people and their everyday life in the first half of the twentieth century was of such importance to the nation's heritage that they established a centre, a museum, a theatre and an exhibition space in which to collate them.

The Life Review and the Grief Review

This desire to form a complete picture in a way that gives new significance and meaning to one's life is the same process that arises spontaneously when one is confronted by death. When a loss occurs, we are immediately flooded with memories of the entire relationship with all its positive qualities and all its difficulties. This is the raw material of grief. Our memory searches for what was not communicated or brought to completion in the relationship and continues to work on evaluating this material from the unconscious until there is resolution. This review is at its most intense and most detailed immediately following the death of someone close to us. That is why most people in grief want and need to talk about the death, the circumstances surrounding the death, and their relationship with that person or event immediately following the loss, for they are beginning their own automatic grief review process. The play *Kids' Stuff* (see Chapter 5) is the grief review of the eight-year old friend of Marcel. As a species, we naturally seek completeness and whole pictures. The plays, films, and literature from which we gain the most enjoyment are those that allow us to be actively involved. As playwright Jeffrey Sweet noted: 'Our goal as playwrights is to engage the audience in our characters and their dilemmas. The way to get an audience engaged is to stimulate them to fill in for themselves what is left unsaid.'[16] So it is with grief. Grief is an active process, not a passive one. As soon as a person in grief becomes aware of this natural review process going on inside them, the work can begin with such simple questions as those posed by James and Friedman, 'What do you wish had been different, better or more?'[17] This work is necessary for our mental, emotional, physical, and spiritual health.

It ensures that we continue to remember our loved ones as we knew them in the fullness of their life, rather than allowing painful memories of how they died or any anger at the circumstances surrounding the death to superimpose themselves upon happier recollections and consume us; it is designed to help us not be frightened of our grief; and it means that as we emerge from our period of mourning, we continue to have a life of significance, value and input, even though our lives have been radically, dramatically, and irrevocably altered.

The Work of Grief

Is there anything that you still want to say to that person that you didn't say in the past?

Is there anything you would have done differently?

How do you know if grief is unresolved?

Unresolved grief is the sand still flying in your eyes from a loss that occurred many years ago. Unresolved grief, like other un-resolved actions, takes a person out of the present moment and into conversations with people who are no longer physically there, separating us from current circumstances by perpetually keeping us in a loop of the past. 'Frozen grief' was the term used by Pauline Boss.[18] If someone fears the intense torment of grief and is resistant to thinking or talking about the one who has died or any other trauma or adversity in their life, if they only want to talk about the positive aspects of the relationship or consider only the negative aspects, if thinking about the relationship brings up fears or affectionate recollections become distressful, then, as J. William Worden noted, they may be experiencing unresolved grief. When a minor event triggers an intense grief reaction, when someone is unwilling to move any material possessions belonging to the deceased, when they convey a false euphoria or persistent guilt and lowered self-esteem after the death, when they make radical changes in their lifestyle following a death or when they exclude friends, family members, and/or activities associated with the deceased from their life, it is likely the person still carries unresolved grief.[19]

A sudden or traumatic death, a fatal accident, a terminal illness or murder, can evoke great rage, guilt, shock, disbelief or a desire for revenge. In such cases the process of grief can become obstructed and repressed and cause symptoms similar to post-traumatic stress disorder, including survivor guilt, extreme agitation, intense sensitivity to stimulus, and uncontrolled and unwanted thoughts. When death is connected to issues that are sensitive in the community, such as AIDS or suicide, the person can feel such extreme shame or confusion that they are unable to express what the loss means for them or even allow themselves to be conscious of their feelings. Unresolved grief is Menelaus unable to move from the bay. The solution is for the individual, at some conscious or unconscious level, to lie down with the seals and to be prepared to move through the ensuing chaos. If this is ignored, if a person pulls back from engaging with the pain through fear or believing life will go on as usual, the likelihood is that the grief becomes embedded and rigid, or another death occurs, offering a renewed opportunity to face Proteus.

Grief puts us through the meat grinder. It takes over and floods our lives. When we lose someone to death, observed sociologist Peter Marris, we don't use the verb in the same way as when we lose our car keys.[20] It is more that the ground beneath our feet gives way and we are catapulted into a zone where gravity no longer works. In reclaiming a new pivot point we find a new axis for ourselves. In so doing, we encounter the work of grief.

Notes
1. Quintus Horatius Flaccus, 65-8 BCE.
2. Publius Ovidius Naso, 43 BCE-17 CE.
3. William Shakespeare. 'The Comedy of Errors' (5.1.298-300) in Stephen Greenblatt et al., eds., *The Norton Shakespeare* (New York: W.W. Norton & Company, Inc., 1997), p.728.
4. http://www.ellawheelerwilcox.org/ - accessed 18 November 2016.
5. Ella Wheeler Wilcox, *Poems of Passion* (Belford, Chicago: Clarke & Co., 1884), p.131.
6. *The West Wing* was created by Aaron Sorkin in 1999 and produced by John Wells Productions in Association with Warner Bros. Television.
7. Mark Twain and John S. Tuckey, *Which Was the Dream?: The Mark Twain Papers and Other Symbolic Writings* (Berkeley and Los Angeles: University of California Press, 1967), p.46.
8. Russell Friedman, 'Death of a long term spouse. Legacy of love or monument to misery.' https://www.griefrecoverymethod. com/blog/1994/07/death-long-term-spouse-legacy-love-or-monument-misery - accessed 17 March 2019.
9. Gretel Killeen was interviewed by Margaret Throsby on ABC Radio Classic FM, Australia, 1 December, 2000.

10. Celia J. Orona, 'Temporality and Identity Loss Due to Alzheimer's Disease,' in *Grounded Theory in Practice*, ed. Anselm L. Strauss and Juliet M. Corbin (Thousand Oaks, CA: Sage Publications, 1997), p.182.

11. Steffen Gais and Jan Born. 'Declarative Memory Consolidation: Mechanisms Acting During Human Sleep.' *Learning & Memory 11*, no. 6 (2004): 679-685, p.684.

12. R. N. Butler, 'Recall and Retrospection,' *Journal of the American Geriatrics Society*, no. 11 (1963): 523-529.

13. R.N. Butler, 'The Life Review: An Interpretation of Reminiscence in the Aged,' *Psychiatry* 26 (1963): 65-70.

14. David Haber, 'Life Review: Implementation, Theory, Research, and Therapy,' *International Journal of Aging and Human Development* 63, no. 2 (2006): 153-171; Peter G. Coleman, 'Ageing and Life History: The Meaning of Reminiscence in Late Life,' *The Sociological Review* 37, no. S1 (1989): 120-143.

15. http://www.age-exchange.org.uk/who-we-are/what-is-reminiscence-arts/- accessed 19 November 2016.

16. Jeffrey Sweet, *The Dramatist's Toolkit: The Craft of the Working Playwright* (Portsmouth, N.H.: Heinemann, 1993), p.11.

17. John W. James and Russell Friedman, *The Grief Recovery Handbook* (New York: Harper Collins, 1998), p.61.

18. Pauline Boss, *Ambiguous Loss: Learning to Live with Unresolved Grief* (Cambridge, Massachusetts: Harvard University Press, 1999), p.4.

19. J. William Worden, *Grief Counseling and Grief Therapy: A Handbook for the Mental Health Practitioner*, 2nd ed. (Springer Publishing Co, 1991), pp.75-77.

20. Peter Marris. *The Politics of Uncertainty: Attachment in Private and Public Life*. London: Routledge, 1996, p.47.

3
A Normal Life

If we could read the secret history of our enemies, we
should find in each man's life sorrow and suffering
enough to disarm all hostility.
  - Henry Wadsworth Longfellow, poet (1807-1882)

In an effort to find out what a 'normal' life looked like,
between March 2000 and April 2003 I undertook qualitative
research, talking with people about their grief using semi-
structured interviews of an hour and half in length based
on a questionnaire in *The Grief Recovery Handbook*.[1] I also
distributed questionnaires at my lectures on grief, stressing
that people's history, their feelings and their precious
memories were valuable to me and that there was no
judgement involved. I asked those who wished to partake
in the questionnaire to write down their earliest memory.
This was a starting point only to stimulate recall, but I
was surprised when this, too, yielded useful information.
Next, I asked them to identify their most painful loss and
to write a paragraph on the circumstances surrounding the
loss and their responses to that loss: How did people try
to help them through that experience? Did they? Could
they? What strategy did they use to gain short-term relief?
The next step was for them to revisit their past and recount
loss events as they remembered them. I asked them to use
a horizontal line to represent linear time and vertical lines
to establish the relative degrees of their losses. I also asked

them to list any substances they used for short-term relief or any short-term behaviour which helped them cope with the pain. I was aware that I was getting a biased sample, as only those people who were prepared to consider their history of loss and grief would be interested in completing such a survey. What follows are two responses.

CASE STUDY: MARGARET
Margaret's history of loss

Earliest memory – 1957 (3 years old):

Playing with buttons.

December, 1959 (5 years old):

Operation on aorta. I was born with a hole in the aorta, near the heart. This caused a lack of oxygenated blood circulating. Consequently I was exceptionally weak. Towards my fifth birthday it became clear I was dying but an operation had been developed in 1958 to correct the condition. I'm aware now that my parents did all they could to explain it to me, but I must not have understood. I thought I'd been left at the hospital for punishment and didn't know what I'd done wrong. I was scared but, more than anything, I was sad that I wasn't good enough for them and when they came to visit me I tried my hardest to be good. I remember lying to a nurse who asked me what was wrong. I don't think I could have put it into words and I know I said nothing to my parents because my mother cried when I told her about it many years later. I remember being given ice-cream if I was good about being in the oxygen tent. A theme of self-medication with food is recurrent in my life.

1971 (17 years old): First incidence of depression

I was working in the Candy Bar of the theatre where my mother worked as an usherette. I had my long hair up and Mum was looking down at me from the upper level. When I got home she told me not to wear my hair scraped back because I looked so plain. I went and looked at myself in the mirror, and she was right. I was, and am, a short, fat, plain person who wears glasses, not at all what any teenage girl wants to be. I was rigid with anger for the next two days because I thought it was so unfair. I hadn't really thought much about looks before, but once I did, I started to hate myself. The anger subsided into depression because I thought that how I looked was going to blight my life. I thought I was unlovable. What I felt I lost was an image of myself as a reasonable looking person. How do I respond to grief? Well, self-pity is one of my strong suits. I went on one of many diets. I still looked like me, only a bit thinner. I don't think anyone knew how I felt and I didn't tell anyone.

April, 1979 (24 years old): First encounter with death

This was the first death I ever experienced. She was my brother's dog, but I loved her and could express it by patting her and looking after her. I felt she loved me, too, and all she asked was to be fed, walked and loved. In a way she was my first love, the first living being to whom I felt I could show affection. Mum rang me at work. I had to behave properly, so I don't remember crying for her then. I tend to bottle things up, eat too much and get depressed in response to loss. After eighteen months, I finally told someone. I went to the Doctor and received anti-depressants.

This was the first death Margaret had experienced and, sadly, her grief was felt for the first living being to whom she could show true affection. If she had been given the opportunity to talk about her brother's dog and her feelings of loss and rage, she may have avoided sliding into depression. Dealing with her grief clearly and openly could possibly have unlocked other, deeper issues about feeling intimidated and unloved. As a result, when later faced with other losses, she may well have responded in a completely different way.

The loss of an animal friend

The loss of an animal friend is a grief many people encounter, yet they often don't pay it the attention it deserves. When we have lived with and cared for an animal for a number of years and been the recipient of its unconditional love, its playfulness, and its companionship, the loss of that component in our lives will be deeply felt. This has begun to be recognised by the pet insurance industry. On Friday 3 May 2002, More Than, part of The Royal & Sun Alliance insurance group, announced its new policy on pet insurance. Already claiming twelve percent of the UK pet insurance market and offering acupuncture and herbal remedies for pets as part of its cover, More Than added a free, twenty-four-hour counselling service staffed by twenty-six counsellors trained by the British Association of Counselling and Psychotherapy specifically for cat and dog owners whose pets became seriously ill or died. Recognising that people share their lives with an animal friend for approximately ten-to-fifteen years and sometimes longer, the company understood that the serious illness or death of such an animal friend was an extremely traumatic event, particularly if the person lived alone. Indeed one in ten claims on More Than's pet insurance products related to an animal's death. Now most pet insurances offer a bereavement helpline, along with a range of agencies in the UK such as Animal Samaritans Pet Bereavement Service, Association of Private Pet Cemeteries and Crematoria, Cats Protection Bereavement Support, EASE Pet Loss Support Services, and Pet Bereavement Support Service.

None of this happened for Margaret at age twenty-four, however, and the unarticulated feelings, which she recognised as powerful and intense, were regarded as trivial by her mother and so Margaret repressed them. Although conscious of how great a part of her twenty-four years of life had been enriched by the unconditional love she had received from her brother's dog, still she was unable to talk about this to anyone for eighteen months. Once more, she comfort ate and put on weight. When she did finally visit a doctor and tried to talk to him about her feelings, he misread her state for depression and prescribed antidepressants, rather than suggesting she seek counselling. Neither of them understood Margaret needed to be given the space to talk more fully about her grief.

December 1995 (41 years old): Grandmother dies

My grandmother was ninety-five when she died. Up until a fall at the age of ninety-two she had been wonderfully fit, active and witty. She kept all her senses up until the day she died, but she couldn't walk for the last three years. In those three years I watched Nanna die by degrees. My grieving for her was done before and after each visit to the Nursing Home. Watching someone you love humiliated, humbled, incapacitated,

bullied, and frightened by those supposedly caring for
them is hard, but far harder for the person living it.
She bore it with grace and dignity. I felt guilty that I
wasn't caring for her, I hated having to go and see her
in the home, and I became frightened of growing old.
These were all part of grief. I discussed it with Mum
sometimes and she felt the same. When she died, I
was calm because her death had been happening in
front of our eyes for so long and it was finally ended. I
hope she is at peace. My response was to eat. I put on
twenty pounds.

Margaret's grandmother's death was part of the natural
life changes that we all encounter. Although the way her
grandmother was treated in aged care in the last three years
of her life frightened her, what stood out for Margaret
amidst the recognition of life's impermanence, its fragility,
and ephemerality was her grandmother's wit and grace.
This was at a point when Margaret needed someone to
listen as she gently opened the door to her grief; someone
who could help her understand her longing for emotional
security, who could place the way her family dealt with loss
into a clear framework, and who could give her insights as
to why she felt outraged by the treatment her grandmother
received and so betrayed by her death. Then she could
have found more effective ways of managing her anger,
frustration and feelings of intimidation, and started to see
herself as loveable. Unpacking all those issues would then
have influenced how she handled her father's death in July
1996 and her mother's operation two months afterwards.
She would then have been able to take a risk and reach out
to other people for what she needed.

July 1996 (41 years old): Father's death

Dad had suffered a series of mini-strokes since mid-1990. After a major stroke left him unable to walk and without much speech, he had to go into a Nursing Home. How I hate those places! Dad sometimes believed he was back in the Army and he wanted to be demobbed or he'd cry to come home. I watched a man I'd feared as a child and despised as a teenager become helpless, lost and miserable. I stopped hating him. I pitied him and then found I loved him. When he died, my grief was different. I got to know about how hard his upbringing was and why he'd been the way he was. I was and am sorry that I spent so much time hating an extremely unhappy man. This sounds so arrogant, but I think I learned about understanding and forgiveness. I told my friends that my Dad had died and many came to his funeral to support me. I don't think I'd realised what good friends I had. After my father's death I ate.

September, 1996 (41 years old): Mother's operation

For over thirty years Mum has been ill with tachycardia (an abnormally rapid heart rate) due to extra 'wiring' to the heart. There had not been a cure until about 1994. Mum said that she felt she couldn't go on, that her heart was failing, so she underwent the operation to burn away the extra nerves to the heart. It had considerable dangers and I was afraid I'd lose her. I started to grieve when I saw her in hospital because I didn't know if I'd see her again. The illness made her thoroughly irritable and naturally she was afraid, too. It was like a reversal of my operation as a five year old.

> I felt helpless that there was nothing I could do to
> influence that most important outcome. I didn't say
> much to anyone about it but boy, I ate a lot.

In this first year after her grandmother's death, in this
time of disorganisation, her unexpressed anger at the
domineering repression she experienced as a child had,
through a crisis of faith, given her insight and compassion:
'I watched a man I'd feared as a child and despised as a
teenager become helpless and lost and miserable. I stopped
hating him. I pitied him and then found I loved him.' This
confrontation with her beliefs continued with her mother's
illness. Nevertheless, still fearful of turning the key in the
lock of her grief, Margaret's reaction was to close down on
communication and to eat.

January 2003 (48 years old): Ray, a good friend of many years, died suddenly at home at the age of eighty-one

> Ray's death is the 'best' I have experienced, in a way.
> He was at home and, though physically rather frail,
> was still in full command of body and mind. He sat
> down to address an envelope, wrote on the front, then
> turned it over to put the sender address and died. He
> was an old fashioned gentleman and scholar and his
> dying at home, in the company of his devoted wife,
> with no great indignities of body and mind attendant
> upon his death, to me is the best way anyone could go.
> While I was surprised by his death, I felt philosophi-
> cal. He'd reached a good age and lived a good life and
> was happy with his life. I feel the usual regrets that I
> had not made more time in the usual 'busyness' of life
> to listen to him more, but I'm glad I knew him. What
> has been surprising is his wife's reaction and how I

react to that. She is hysterically, furiously angry at him
for leaving her. She is eighteen years younger than him
and has been deeply devoted, to the point where her
life has been curtailed by his weakness and inability
to do much. She had spoken of the minor irritations
and limitations of her life with him and I knew she
resented it somewhat, but had no idea she would be so
angry. Her words on trying to find something amongst
his many collections: 'I shouldn't have to do this! It
shouldn't be like this!' What's relevant here is that I
have little understanding of her reaction and, I regret,
little sympathy. While I say all the formulaic things to
her and generally just provide a listening ear, privately
I think she is being ungrateful. She has been left
extremely well provided for, he expressed his love to
her every day, he always thanked her for her good care,
and took the greatest interest and pride in her activities outside the home. I know I don't know everything
about their life together, but, deep down, I find her
reaction somewhat repugnant.

Rage has been an odd theme of reaction to the
death of such a gentle man, but it has had this affect
on me, too, in another way. At work (I was working
in Payroll), it was made extremely difficult for me to
attend Ray's funeral. I had no choice but to shut the
office and put a sign on the door (in my view, tanta-
mount to deserting the ship!) The other three work
colleagues were either on leave or insisting they had
to be somewhere else and this time I refused to carry
the can. As usual, the rage burned brightly inside, but
was not expressed externally until later. I wrote out
my resignation and held onto it until I could arrange

my finances. Although I intended to give five weeks' notice so they could employ a replacement, in the end I couldn't contain the anger and left after three weeks. I'd started to tell friends how annoyed I was and, encouraged by their support, just left. Drawing a not-too-long bow, I ran away in response.

February 2003 (48 years old): My Aunt Doreen (father's sister) died, after a year of suffering pancreatic cancer

Like my father, she was an unhappy and bitter person all her life. She used to terrify us kids with sudden inexplicable screaming rages. I know now that her parents visited their sins upon the children: their father was a brute and their mother embittered and vindictive. The sudden rages were a feature of both Dad and Doreen and I'd say rage is a big theme in the family: depression is submerged rage. I'm ashamed to admit I was sick of visiting hospitals and Nursing Homes, and was (unexpressedly) angry that, for the third time in six years, I had to do it all again. I struggled with the sense of duty and some empathy, against the wish for a life where this wasn't the pattern. Oh, yes, I ate. Put back the stone in weight I'd lost.

I had spoken to friends about Doreen and they were sympathetic, but there's a lot you can't say, like: 'God, please, no one else is allowed to die!!! I never want to see another @#*&! ruddy Nursing Home again, I'll kill myself before I get too old, so it can't happen to me.' Fear of getting old is a boiling undercurrent in how I felt. When she died, I was sad for her wasted life, but relieved that it was over. Mostly I feel sorry for her. She never enjoyed her life

and I don't want to be like that. Doreen left me her
house, which I am selling. I know I should be grateful
and I'm sure I will be when I realise the money. I am,
however, deeply ashamed that I resent the burdens
attendant upon this, as the house is something of a
white elephant. While I discuss practicalities with
friends and they have been extremely helpful and kind,
which is much appreciated, there is a lot left unsaid.

For a while I was in stasis, in a way, just waiting for
the next blow to fall. Then it fell.

**April, 2003 (48 years old): A good friend was diagnosed
with cancer and then my cousin Sally, fifty-two years
old, had a major stroke at work, is on a ventilator, and
still unconscious after four days**

In this case I have less obligation to visit the hospital
and haven't gone. What can I say or do for her in this
state? I'm forty-eight years old. Sally's situation is a
much closer object lesson for me. I know I should be
working on making my life worthwhile, but I'm stuck.
Every muscle is tense and I'm so tired I find moving an
effort. My feelings are: 'Please can this stop? Please can
there be some fun and happiness? No more dying.'

Mum is now in better health than she has enjoyed
in thirty years, which she freely acknowledges. Mum
and I are close, but still many things go unsaid. She is
an unsentimental person and I'm all watery emotion,
so sometimes we don't quite mesh. Still, couldn't get
by without my Mum, as the ads say!

Right now I'm a lady of leisure and though I've
been invited to return to my old job, am doing some
serious thinking on how to make more out of my

life, to put meaning into the experience of working.

Doreen's and Sally's examples are strong in my mind.

From Margaret's perspective, she was caught in a paradoxical loop. She felt that Ray's death at home at the age of eighty-one 'in full command of body and mind' had been a good death, yet she was enraged when her colleagues made it difficult for her to attend his funeral. She resented the responsibility of having to visit her aunt in a Nursing Home, yet she understood she had gained financial freedom as the inheritor of her aunt's house. When, in April, her friend was diagnosed with cancer and a cousin, close to her in age, had a stroke and was left in a coma, Margaret manifested the stresses of this period through her body as tense muscles and tiredness.

Proteus had visited Margaret in many different forms in her life. Sometimes she was able to move towards him as he lay down with the seals, but mostly she pulled away and covered her emotional distress with eating: 'I know I should be working on making my life worthwhile, but I'm stuck.' This was Menelaus in a windless harbour, trapped in grief and without a solution. This would have been an appropriate time for her to look deeply at what governed her life, to shake loose the coils of rage and bitterness and approach ageing in a constructive and joyful way. This was a time when she could have taken action to reshape her life and hone old skills in order to gain success. The difficulty was that the lack of air in the bay was now oppressive and binding and the urge to continue as a by-product of her family, rather than as a freshly-generated blossom, was overwhelming.

CASE STUDY : XENA
Xena's history of loss

Earliest memory – 1963 (6 years old)

Half the class got strapped by the nuns because we accepted lollies from the local priest. I remember being confused and upset because I couldn't work out what we had done wrong, since we'd all been laughing at the tricks the priest was doing for us.

Emergent Pattern

Xena's earliest memory was one of active punishment and pain for accepting kindness (the lollies). Unable to defend herself verbally, she experienced rejection, affecting her developing ego and identity. It left an indelible memory of betrayal by an authority figure for an act of innocence.

29 September, 1965 (nearly 8 years old): Grandfather dies

Mum told me that Poppa, her father, had died and that she and Dad were going to Berry, a little town on the south coast of New South Wales, Australia, where Mum was born and brought up, to go to the funeral. I wondered why I couldn't go and I remember Mum being sensible about the whole thing, but I also remember sensing her grief, though I didn't understand it at the time. My mother adored her father.

First encounter with grief – what was being planted

Being 'sensible about the whole thing' was Xena's first encounter with how adults grieved. No-one talked about the deep worry and anguish catalysed by her grandfather's death that Xena instinctively felt from her mother. Nor was she allowed to go to the funeral. Surrounded by silence, she learnt to disregard her feelings and isolate herself. The boat slows, the wind dies. Menelaus is becalmed in the bay. A metaphorical hole began to form in the pattern of Xena's psyche.

1970 (12 years old): Diabetes Mellitus type 'I'

In Australia, primary, secondary and tertiary school
years begin in February. When I was about to start
high school, I developed diabetes mellitus type 'I'.
I was so sick and out of it that I didn't really realize
what was happening to me. I just did what I was
told, as I'd always done because I was always scared
that I would do something wrong. I do remember
the shock, though, of a nurse walking in one day
and telling me I had to give myself injections from
now on. (Since I'd been a small child I've always been
terrified of injections. I still am which is pretty bizarre
when I have more than eight needles going into my
body each day and, to put it bluntly, I suppress all
the emotion around this particular can of worms. I'm
scared that if I think about it too much I will give up.)
I'm sure people tried to help and my parents probably
were there for me, or at least Mum was, but I don't
remember them being there. I don't remember being
comforted or held as all these terrible things were
happening to my body. I just remember always being
alone with this trip.

How did I gain short-term relief? There is no
short-term relief with this. It's with me every second of
every minute of every day and night of my life. I suppress my feelings towards it, I try not to think about
it, I try to be sensible, I try not to become obsessed,
I try to be 'normal', I try to be brave and strong just

like my mother taught me — and this doesn't work. At that time I would have been confused and I would have tried to be a brave little girl.

In the winter (June-July-August) I was so sick I started to go into a death coma. Mum and Dad were about to go overseas. I tried to tell my mother all winter that something was wrong. It was a truly horrible time. Anyway nothing happened until one day I couldn't walk anymore and my parents rang the doctor and I remember Dad carrying me into hospital. I was drugged and out of it and that in itself was a relief for awhile, until I was back in the real world again.

Loss of health

The potential health difficulty in her childhood had now become apparent. Although she was about to start high school, with its offer of authority, credibility, and respect in the wider community, instead her status was renamed 'diabetic' and her separation anxiety was exacerbated: 'I don't remember being comforted or held as all these terrible things were happening to my body.' Scared that she might do something wrong, she suppressed her feelings and did as she was told. The pattern of how to deal with loss was reinforced: 'I try to be sensible, I try not to become obsessed, I try to be "normal", I try to be brave and strong just like my mother taught me.' A hole called 'loss of health' formed in her psyche and it connected with the first hole called 'don't talk about Poppa's death', only now the consequences took one step closer and manifested in her own body. The first piece of the jigsaw puzzle fell out of the pattern, and the ship did not stir in the bay.

6 January, 1979 (21 years old): Death of best friend

I lost one of my best friends, Paul. (My other friend at the time was my younger brother, Patrick.) Paul's death was a rather remote event. He was killed in a motorbike accident. His parents rang to let me know what had happened, but there was no funeral or wake or anything. Paul's family closed down and kept everything within the immediate household. I didn't get to see his parents until much later.

At this time I was in a highly destructive relationship that had begun in 1978 with a man called Thaddeus. In the period after Paul's death, Thaddeus' father had repeatedly attempted to commit suicide and Thaddeus was getting fed up with picking up the pieces afterwards to the point where he wished that if his father was going to kill himself, then the least he could do was do it properly. I was now drinking heavily and occasionally smoking dope and hashish.

I can't remember what I did about Paul's death, however, and it wasn't until a few years ago that I went and found where his ashes were buried. I probably suppressed it all, as was my habit well and truly by then — like, I'm standing here functioning in the world like a socially and politically correct robot because my feelings and my emotions and my real thoughts are well buried and by this stage in my life what's buried has become too, too threatening.

Loss of companionship

Xena was twenty-one years old. Not helped by Paul's family physically and emotionally distancing her from the event, once again Xena suppressed her emotions. The embedded pattern of rejection and isolation was reinforced. She learnt to put on a socially acceptable face to the world, but underneath, the real issues were hidden and strangled. She learnt not to ask for help to deal with her unresolved grief, which was now beginning to compound. More holes were formed in the jigsaw. More pieces of the pattern were lost. No wind was predicted in the bay.

24 February 1980 (22 years old): Most painful loss

I was with my younger brother, Patrick, when he was killed in a motorbike accident on 24 February, 1980. It was a strange day. Patrick was helping Thaddeus and I move house. We had just finished the move and had decided to go to a local pub for a counter lunch in the early afternoon. Patrick was on his red motorbike in front of our white Valiant station wagon. The road we were travelling down was a dual carriage way and there were no trees or buildings on the corners which meant the area of vision at each intersection was clear. I was lighting a cigarette when Thaddeus said to me, 'Patrick has been hit', so I didn't see the actual moment of collision. A young man had just finished work and was going home in his car and he didn't see Patrick as he came through the intersection. There was no speed involved in the accident. It was just the way the contact happened and the way Patrick fell on the ground — his head hit the edge of the concrete curb. I figure he must have broken his neck on impact because when I got to him there was no visible damage, just a trickle of blood coming out of his nose, but I knew he was dying. The strange thing is that if he had fallen about an inch or two further onto the nature strip he would have been okay, if a bit battered and bruised. The poor

young man that hit him came up to me and asked
me who I was and when I told him, he cracked up. I
remember my heart breaking for him because he was
young and all he had been doing was going home after
work on a Saturday afternoon and I couldn't imagine
what it would be like to know that, for the rest of
your life, just because you didn't check an intersection
properly, you ended up killing someone. I sometimes
wondered how it affected his life. So there was no
blame, only grief and sorrow.

My immediate emotional response was, 'This is
not true, this is not possible, this sort of thing doesn't
happen to me, it only happens to other people'. And
then this circular steel wall came down through the
centre of my being and I went numb. I went to the
hospital in the ambulance. I went to the morgue to
identify the body. Then I went to my parents' house
and I realized so clearly that there would be no support or refuge there and that, for the first time in my
life, I really was on my own to get through this. People
were kind and generous, doing the Irish Catholic
thing. I am the eldest child in the family, but Patrick
was the eldest son, but all I remember is being told I
had to be strong and brave, for my parents and for my
siblings and all I wanted to do was scream, 'Don't you
realize what I've just seen?' (and as I write this I can
still feel it inside me).

I remember seeing the photographs from the
funeral at dinner at my parents' place one night and I
began to cry and my mother told me to stop … and
now, twenty years later, I realize that if I had have
cracked that night, the dam of grief and unexpressed

emotion that the family was holding back god only knows for how many generations would have burst and that was too terrifying. So I tried to get relief by trying to live life, trying hard to function normally and I began to die inside. How did I deal with it? I didn't. I drank, Thaddeus used to roll me a joint at night to help me sleep, and sex.

My parents seemed to separate out of their relationship after Patrick died. Both of them locked themselves into their own world of grief. I remember talking to Dad one night out on the driveway, just before I went home to my place. I asked him why he and Mum didn't talk to each other about what had happened to Patrick and share their grief and support each other emotionally. He told me that Mum had her way of dealing with things and he had his. I remember feeling incredibly sad at this and thinking that a marriage, a relationship, should be more than two emotionally separate individuals living together under the one roof. Dad and Mum are both extremely devout Roman Catholics. After Patrick died Mum went right into her faith and drew strength from it, and Dad almost lost his faith in the church and God.

Death of brother

Xena's initial responses to her brother's death were normal and natural: pain, shock, numbness, and disbelief. The problem occurred when the family had the opportunity to express their shared grief and it was suppressed: 'I had to be strong and brave ... and all I wanted to do was scream.' Later when she attempted to discuss her distress with her mother (seeing the photographs from the funeral at dinner at her parents' place), her mother blocked her. Life now demanded that she change and redefine her philosophy, but did not take into account the constraints of a family who did not want to deal with grief. Struggling to be heard, Xena's emotions were smothered with alcohol, drugs, and sex in an effort to stop the pain. By now the jigsaw had many holes missing. The unconscious picture was fragmenting badly and Menelaus was slowly starving in the bay.

1982 (24 years old): Leave family

I dropped out of university. I failed myself, I failed my mother, I failed my father. By this stage of my life depression had become a constant companion. I was sick all of the time because my diabetes was out of control (my diabetes has always been unstable, it's just a matter of degrees), therefore I was on an emotional roller coaster and some part of me knew I was dying because parts of me had stopped working: digestion, menstrual cycle, lymphatic and elimination systems. Still I kept trying to be normal and get it together … I just kept working and drinking. I left Canberra and went to live in an ashram an hour's drive north of Sydney. In retrospect this was a huge move. I left my family, I left my culture, I left my socioeconomic group and I left my religious upbringing (which had pretty much gone by that time anyway). I found short-term relief in dealing with the new environment, especially as an insulin-dependent diabetic, and work, and I worked between twelve and twenty hours a day for the next thirteen-to-sixteen years.

Two side effects of diabetes mellitus are hair loss and retinal haemorrhaging. At that time my hair was

falling out in clumps, so in 1983 it was easy to decide
to have my head shaved as I thought it would help
my hair grow. Retinal haemorrhaging means the cells
on the retina leak blood into the vitreous fluid in the
eye, and so the space between the lens and the retina
becomes opaque. For quite a few years the ophthal-
mologists who were treating me thought I was going
to lose my eyesight. It was horrible because I'd wake
up each morning and be too scared to open my eyes
just in case I couldn't see anything. The treatment is
to burn off the cells that are leaking with laser in order
to arrest the development of the haemorrhaging. I got
to the point where I hated the treatment as much as
my fear of going blind. The haemorrhaging increased
from 1986 onwards and reached its climax during
1991-1993. As of late 2000 that is now in recession
and has been for five or six years. One thing I learnt in
this period is that the medical profession rarely tell the
whole truth. People kept telling me that it was all going to be okay and to just keep on going as if nothing
was happening and to think beautiful thoughts (this
one came from my father), but it was pretty hard when
I only had partial vision in either one or both eyes and
no sense of depth.

Secondary symptoms
The suppressed and denied grief now revealed itself through
secondary symptoms: depression, problems with digestion,
menstrual cycle, lymphatic and elimination systems. As if
sensing changes ahead of her, Xena broke her commitment
to University education and sought a new teaching
body in the shape of an ashram. She wanted to gain an

understanding of her identity through a guru, but instead of dealing with her suppressed emotions, she went into overdrive with work. Hard work and drink, however, are only short-term reprieves, the ill-informed ways of a world focused on visible productivity and, in the final analysis, powerless to compensate for buried issues.

1996 (38 years old): Leaves ashram/undermined by family

I was in India for about a month at the end of 1995 for a tantric ceremony that extended over two weeks, devoted to the feminine force of the universe. At the same time I witnessed the ceremony of initiation of a tantric guru. By the time that I returned to Australia I knew that I could no longer remain in the ashram because I couldn't handle the hypocrisy anymore. This loss was a way of life that had held so much potential for me, yet the underbelly of the spiritual world had been so disillusioning. So in January or February 1996 I asked my mother and father if I could stay with them for a while until I sorted myself out. My father wanted to help me. My mother didn't want to know about me. And so began a devastating seven-to-nine months living with my mum and dad and a sister who had never moved out of home. The loss this time was my already non-existent sense of self-worth. It was a nightmare. It was a nightmare that I intellectually knew I could get out of, yet some part of me couldn't or didn't want to. The situation culminated with the four of us sitting down and my father telling me I had to leave because I didn't fit in and that all the tension in the house was because of me. This was the most

devastating thing that has ever happened to me and
I still cry when I think about it. I felt I had no place
in the world or in the universe and that I was worth-
less. I felt so unloved. What did I do? I shut down
emotionally yet again and just kept going because
that was what I had always done. If I thought beyond
what I had to do next, then I think I would have killed
myself, that's how much this one got to me, even more
than being with Patrick while he died.

About four weeks after this discussion I visited the
ashram because someone was out from India. Four
weeks after this I had packed up my life in Australia
and went to live and work in India indefinitely. As far
as I was concerned, the further away I was from my
family, the better. In India any lingering illusions I had
about gurus and spiritual life were destroyed. I worked
and tried to keep my diabetic body together. That
took most of my energy until I realized that if I stayed
much longer I would not survive another summer over
there. Part of me really wanted to die and part of me
really wanted to live and part of me was addicted to
the drama of all this.

Loss of self-worth

Once again Xena had to deal with her siblings and family
at a close level. Instead of protection, however, she became
the family scapegoat and encountered despair. Isolation
had now become Xena's permanent way of dealing with
grief: 'The further away I was from my family the better.'
Amongst this devastation, the recognition that life was
finite and that she, Xena, was mortal, attempted to make
itself heard. What Xena had begun to realise was that the

far off dream of 'one-day when I grow up — ...' and the belief that life would be easier, more comfortable, more abundant once she moved into the fairy tale land 'in the ever after' was dead. It was this life or nothing.

1997 (39 years old): Death of 'spiritual' teacher

My first 'spiritual' teacher, Swami A., died in June 1997. I heard about his death in India and my reaction to it was anger and rage. I met Swami A. in my early twenties and it was an interaction with him in November 1982 that precipitated my decision to leave Canberra and my family and go and live in an ashram. He promised that he could help me deal with the diabetes. In retrospect this was the beginning of sixteen years of broken promises and shattered dreams, yet paradoxically it probably saved my life, that is, the yogic practices probably saved my physical life but there was a high price to pay. Swami A. was an exceedingly charismatic teacher and he had what it took to become great, but the charisma evaporated when money and power gained an upper hand. He blew it all in about 1986 by embezzling company funds and seducing underage girls and he ended up in prison. Eventually he became an alcoholic and this was the cause of his death. I obviously suppressed my rage and anger at his betrayal of my faith and trust in him for many years until I heard of his death in India in 1997. I was getting out of the lift in the library on my way to work one morning and Jyotirmayananda rushed up to me and said, 'Swami A. has just died.' I just shrugged my shoulders and kept going. A few minutes later when I walked into my office and began

sorting through the work for the day, the rage erupted
from the pit of my abdomen. I was immensely angry
at Swami A., ashrams, gurus, and the whole 'spiritual'
trip. The setting was appropriate because there I was
in India in an ashram working for a guru, when the
guru in question, Swami N., walked through the door.
All I remember is looking at Swami N. and thinking
really clearly, 'You and your guru and your ashrams
are nothing but a con!' It still took me another year to
extricate myself.

Anger

The event that precipitated Xena's decision to leave her
family and go and live in an ashram was meeting Swami A.
Now fifteen years later, this powerful shaping relationship
in her life was dead. She was forced to face and define what
she considered would give her fulfilment or completeness,
aware of the need to change her standing in the community.
What she was left with, however, was once again anger and
a sense of betrayal.

1998 (40 years old): Leaves ashram for the final time

I left the ashram for the last time in May, 1998. This
loss took a while to filter through to my consciousness.
When I had arrived back in Australia, the chairman
and treasurer of the ashram organisation asked if
I would help the board of directors restructure it
administratively and legally. I agreed to help for six
months, which I did. However, the politics in the
ashram, which make federal and state politics look
like child's play, reached a point where I resigned my
position and left. This time I didn't go anywhere near
my family. However, learning to survive in the real

world when you are a forty-year-old, single woman
with no material resources and an unstable physical
body doesn't leave much time to grieve for a way of
life that has consumed sixteen years of your life. In
November or December 1998 I went to the doctor
because of the shocking pains I was having, and am
still having, while I menstruate. At that time the
tests showed atypical cells on the walls of my vagina
and cervix. These were frozen off and recent tests are
clear. The menstrual cramps continue, however, with
vomiting and diarrhoea each month and the allopathic
doctors suggest having a hysterectomy, which I'm not
going to have.

Changes
This was a year of the blinding flash of the obvious, giving
her freedom from her business relationship (the ashram)
and the opportunity to adjust the course of her life. For
Xena, this was a major loss of a way of life, but this time she
chose not to look for emotional support from her family.
Instead her body expressed this loss through a health crisis.

2000 (42 years old): 15 February 2000.
This was the day that Dr White told me that the
insulin injections weren't really effective and asked
whether I could find $6,250 (AUD) to have an insulin
pump installed. The pump costs about $250 (AUD)
a month to maintain with tubing and catheters and
batteries and swabs — all the paraphernalia. Dad paid
for the pump and my friend, Chris, the man with
whom I now have a relationship, helps me out with
my medical costs. I love them both dearly, but I was

really hoping to become financially independent at some point in the near future. Maybe it would be a good idea to let that dream go for a while.

My relationship with Chris began to take on a courting flavour in March 1998 and by the end of that month we had slept together. To put this in perspective, I had known Chris for many years prior to this and had worked with him at different times when he was involved with ashram affairs — even though he has never lived in the ashram. When I got back from India he was one of the two people who approached me to do the secretarial work for the organisation while they were restructuring. This time there was a definite spark between us and he was the person with whom I had to work most closely — although I'm sure both of us engineered it that way. The rest, as they say, is history. As much as any of us can be certain of life's unfolding, we are both in this relationship for the long haul.

17 April, 2000 — 17:55

At Prince of Wales Hospital, Sydney, the catheter was inserted into my body and at 18:00 the pump began pumping — my little lifeline. It has transformed my life.

Early November, 2000

I knew this would be a huge change for me and it proved to be much bigger than I anticipated. Six months after going onto the insulin pump I've become used to the whole thing and so has my body. So the diabetes is easing, but from July onwards I kept getting viral infections and felt exhausted all the time. I had tests done and found out I was anaemic. I hadn't eaten meat for about twenty years and although I'd been taking iron supplements for a couple of years, I hadn't been absorbing them. Things reached such a crisis point that I was prepared to do about anything and last weekend I went and bought a kilo of beef, a cast iron pot, and a bottle of red wine (for me to cope with eating the meat). I braised a big beef stew and I've been eating it each day. I'm beginning to feel much stronger physically and I'm even beginning to enjoy eating it. The one thing that has kept me going this year is my counselling studies, begun in February 2000. It's the one thing that I can feel passionate about and focus on and it helps keep my head out of trouble.

Irrevocable adjustments

Health issues from the past were now the focus for Xena, only this time it gave her solutions. The rejection, isolation and her inability to discuss how she felt were all emphasised. Physical and emotional changes to her body forced her to take on a new level of responsibility: the insulin pump and eating meat. Finally, she gained stability for her body, a stronger sense of self-worth, and a relationship that was both loving and understanding.

26 July 2001 (43 years old): Mother diagnosed with breast cancer

My mother rang from Canberra to say that she had been diagnosed with cancer in her left breast. I flew down to Canberra on 28 July and stayed until 30 July and it was a truly horrible time because all the dysfunctional family dynamics were in full swing, along with all of the unexpressed unresolved grief in my family. It took me weeks to recover from this trip emotionally. Eventually I valued the insights I gained into my own behaviour within my family unit through being there and watching how I reacted to the extreme stress at that time. This, in turn, triggered me into working again with my own dysfunctional behaviour in relationship and now (March 2003), I feel like I am making some headway in being able to hold my own space even when I am with my family. Mum ended up having a lumpectomy. There was only a little bit of cancer there and it had not spread to the lymph nodes.

What did I do to help deal with this internal distress? Telling my story to you and then going through *The Grief Recovery Handbook* took the lid off everything that I had blocked out. I thought about this last night after sending off the last bit of information to you and I feel how important it is to be able to tell my story of my experiences, to have it heard and acknowledged. This is so essential. Beginning to work through my grief has helped to loosen me up a lot, especially my emotionally reactive patterns to people and life. So because I am a little more open now, I begin to notice when I react strongly to certain situations and I begin to wonder why I do so. After that visit to Canberra my naturopath recommended that I see a particular healer in order to start working on an emotional level, mainly because I was feeling really, really stuck with my teaching, despite naturopathic treatment and having acupuncture every week. This, in turn, has led me to work on an energetic level with my relationship with my mother and the rest of my family. The knowl-

edge that I gain from this gives me powerful tools that
help me to shift belief systems and behaviour. I now
feel that I am able to respond to people and situations
rather than being extremely reactive all the time. In
other words, I now tend to ask why I think the way I
do and why I believe the things I do and while this is
an ongoing process, last year and this year there have
been subtle shifts in my relationship with my family
and especially with my mother. It's all slow work and
intense, but that's part of the journey, I suppose. I
hang in there as best I can. I feel deeply and strongly
that filling out your grief questionnaire was the beginning of this healing process for me. Telling stories is
such a powerful medium, as you no doubt know.

Finding her voice for the first time – Proteus reveals himself

The inability of her family to adequately deal with loss
when Xena was young, the pattern she internalised and
adopted, anxious to be accepted, and which kept being
reinforced every time she encountered loss as an adult, was
a metaphorical landmine destined eventually to explode.
Finally, Proteus revealed himself to Xena. 'Telling my
story to you and then going through *The Grief Recovery
Handbook* took the lid off everything that I had blocked
out.' Her sacrifice made, Xena was now free to return home
with wind in her sails.

June, 2002 (44 years old): Loss of night vision

I began to notice that it was becoming harder and
harder for me to drive at night. I reached the point
where I didn't think it was safe, so I made an appointment with my optometrist for 1 August, 2002,

and asked him whether I was being fanciful or was something happening to my eyes. He was horrified that I was driving at night at all and then explained that because the surfaces of both my eyes have been completely lasered in order to prevent me going blind, I am now reaping the side effects of this treatment and have begun to develop something like blind spots on parts of my retina. This felt like a punch in the stomach at the time. How could I go out socially at night and how could I teach yoga at night unless I had someone to ferry me about? Loss of independence is a scary thought to me. It also brought back all of the years I lived in fear, when the possibility of losing my eyesight altogether was really high. Luckily I will always be able to read, but I have lost some of my peripheral vision. It is as if my retina has difficulty receiving images at night if it is happening quickly. If I go from bright daylight into a dark room it takes quite a while, relatively speaking, for my eyes to adjust and the same going from dark into daylight which is painful for me at times.

Once I have adjusted it is usually okay. It is, however, difficult for me to distinguish objects at night. It's like there is not enough contrast for the objects to register on my retinal surface and this, combined with my reduced peripheral vision, makes it dangerous for me to drive. Chris would drive me, even though it is a fair distance from his place, but I am kind of relieved not to do the class at the moment. I am happy to do the two classes I have during the day on Wednesday. This, with the study and students is enough for me at the moment — along with arranging to move in with Chris.

31 March, 2004 (46 years old): Move in with Chris

Well, I passed my counselling exam with a credit,
which I am kind of happy with. It was really strange
adjusting to life without study, but I'm enjoying getting used to it. The relocation took up a lot of that
space. Yes, as of a week ago, the event that has been
going to take place for years happened: I moved in
with Chris. I thought the equinox was a good time to
take the plunge. Chris is surrounded by two hectares
of bush and sandstone on a hill that overlooks euca-
lyptus and bays of water in one direction and out to
the ocean in another. I know I will be happy here. I
feel settled. Our first week of living together was rather
traumatic, as both Chris and I went into our dysfunctional behaviour patterns, provoking and bouncing
off each other. However, even going through that and
even thinking 'oh my god what have I done?', I did,
and do, feel like this move is right and appropriate;
and when I stop still and feel deep into the relationship and the land on which we dwell, I do feel settled.
I feel it in my body and my bones and I feel it in my
inner being — and the feeling is so sweet and pure —
I can't ever remember feeling like this.

2 April, 2004: Yesterday, not long after I sent my
email to you, I was sitting on the train going down
to Sydney and began reflecting again on the move
and the past six months — and I was really proud of
myself. Over the past two years I seem to have travelled an extremely long way because not only had I
managed to sit the exam and pass (which to me was a
huge achievement, given my past history at achieving
for myself), but I have also developed enough sense

of confidence, self-esteem, and self-worth to actually move in with and engage in a full relationship with someone. I can feel my faith in myself welling up inside me and the belief that I have a right to be here on this earth. Two years ago, four or five years ago, such things would have been inconceivable to me. So as I travelled through gorges and watched the Hawkesbury River slip by, I really did think, 'Wow, well done!' And that's the story up until today, a happy ending and a new beginning.

A happy ending

We breathe in to bring oxygen into our systems and we breathe out to release harmful carbon dioxide. We eat and drink to energise and nourish our body. We urinate and defecate to release detritus. The excretory processes of exhaling, urinating, perspiring, defecating, and crying play a vital role in maintaining homeostasis by removing waste and harmful substances and it is no different on an emotional level. We take in sensory experiences by living them, but talking about them, thinking about them, and shaping them into a story that has meaning for us allows us to let go of that which does us harm. For Xena, being able to tell her story released the valve that had remained tightly closed for decades. She proactively engaged with processing what all of these losses meant for her and reached out for life with Chris in their new home on the Hawkesbury River. In so doing, one can argue that she added ten years to her life. In 2006 Xena developed breast cancer. She approached this news resolutely and optimistically and held the cancer in check until 2010 when she developed secondaries. Xena died early in the morning of 4 December 2011.

What these loss histories tell us

Margaret's and Xena's loss histories are not stand-alone narratives. In hearing other people's histories of loss and the circumstances around their grief, a universal truth became clear, that while life may appear to deal more harshly with some people than with others, all our lives are filled with losses. Further, if these losses are unresolved, when people recalled these sad events, it was with intensity, vividness, and great emotion. These memories were as alive and painful as if they had happened last week. Additionally, the reactions of parents to a child's early losses, such as the death of a pet or a grandparent, decided the pathway for future losses. Rather than parents seeing such events as portals through which grief and the corresponding emotions that accompany it could be discussed and managed, the common response was to suppress or silence the child. Furthermore, when issues inside the family unit became too difficult, they were projected onto a member of the family and splits occurred. A 'normal' family in the twentieth and twenty-first centuries is one that contains cut-offs, detachments, splits, and the withheld anger of generations past. Finally, in most cases, it was not until after a person had turned thirty and sometimes well into their late-thirties to early-forties, that they could start to gain some sort of perspective on how they had been suppressing feelings of grief.

Parents imprint onto their children a spectrum of possibilities of how to manage emotions and relate to others, along with how to be in the world and take responsibility for their lives. The manner in which early losses are handled has a serious impact on how they manifest in an adult. There is also no guarantee that the natural maturation process of the adult will alter the way they handle their grief unless they actively engage with the process. Margaret was able to find a way through the maze to fully grieve when, at forty-one years old, she finally saw her father through adult eyes. She was able to talk about the death with her friends and allow them to support her. Xena was able to release the valve of bottled grief at the age of forty-three by telling me her story.

Other women gave me similar responses. Shelley told me that when her father died when she was seven-and-a-half years old, she was 'excluded from the process by my mother and therefore the rest of my family, thinking that I did not understand what was happening'. At the age of seventeen she watched her mother struggle with her step-father's death. At the age of eighteen she experienced the death of her sister's youngest child just after childbirth. At the age of nineteen she had to handle her uncle's death alone as the family no longer kept in touch with him. It wasn't until the age of thirty-two, when her ten -year old nephew was killed in an accident, that she began to recognise the pattern:

> My brother and wife and two of his three daughters, along with his son, were in the car. This was a highly traumatic time for the whole family and I had difficulty dealing with this as no-one was prepared to communicate their grief. For the first time I realised that this was how we dealt with tragedy, by pretending it wasn't happening. My role with my mother reversed and I became the nurturer, trying to help her come to terms with the situation. As I was unable to discuss the situation within my family, I turned to reading books as I struggled to understand why a ten-year old child could be taken

from us so suddenly, looking for the answer to 'why did this happen?' There must be a reason.

Catherine told me that at the age of thirty-five, she realised that exercise was a useful valve to release anger and she also began attending counselling sessions. Miranda told me that she was in her late thirties before she felt able to resist previous patterns of getting drunk and stoned to deal with her grief and started to face the feelings inside her. Normalising grief doesn't diminish its importance. It means accepting all of the emotions associated with the pain and managing them at the time they occur so they can create resources for future losses.

Conclusion

Breath, like air, has heat energy, kinetic energy and pressure. For Menelaus and his wind-starved sailors, there was nothing lyrical about the lazy slap of wave against hull, the rock of a ship going nowhere. The leap from stranded to lifeless is only a matter of breathing. It is one of the body's vital signs. Marooned in the bay, the pressure rises from miserable to intolerable, but to whom could Menelaus turn? In this commercial and industrial age we have learnt 'lean-back technology'. We distance ourselves and use clichés and platitudes to push away people in grief. 'Lean-forward technology' is the demanding skill of listening with an open heart, without judgement or blame and with consideration. Xena's statement was simple enough: '... how important it is to be able to tell my story of my experiences, to have it heard and acknowledged.' In *Macbeth* when Macduff learns of the savage slaughter of his wife and children, Malcolm implores him:

What, man, ne'er pull your hat upon your brows.
Give sorrow words. The grief that does not speak
Whispers the o'erfraught heart and bids it break.[2]

To allow someone in grief to give voice to their experiences is not just being kind. It is saving their life.

Notes

1.   John W. James and Russell Friedman, *The Grief Recovery Handbook* (New York: Harper Collins, 1998), Chapter 5, pp.85-102.
2.   William Shakespeare. 'Macbeth' (4.3.209-211) in Stephen Greenblatt et al., eds. *The Norton Shakespeare*. New York: W.W. Norton & Company, Inc., 1997, p.2607.

4

A Way Through the Dark – Parents in Grief

When it is dark enough, you can see the stars.
- Ralph Waldo Emerson (1803-1882)

Grief is a long term process and its objective is to help facilitate healing. While we cannot change events that have already taken shape and passed us by, we can change our attitude towards the past, which then changes our attitude towards future events. In the immediacy of the loss, in the grip of unspeakable, illogical confusion, we want someone who can tell us that our feelings of aloneness and pain will end. More importantly, what we need is someone who will hear our story, won't patronise us, and will understand the excruciating pain we are now feeling.

Family dynamics and life expectancy
There are two other factors that enter into people's lives during grief: the first is family dynamics and what happens to these when death strikes; the second is an understanding of life expectancy.

Family dynamics
Families are naturally fractured units. They gather for a time and condense around a central core, but like gravel they are also composed of different material: some parts mix well, others don't. Eventually, like all living things that

produce seeds, those seeds fly in the wind. The core of the family separates and a nucleus forms elsewhere.

This coagulation around a central core which fluxes for a time and then breaks apart and begins the dance elsewhere, is mirrored in a mathematical creation called The Game of Life, invented by mathematician John Conway in 1970.[1] He developed this game as a simple way of studying patterns and behaviours in complex systems. The Game revealed whether a pattern will die out completely, form a stable population or grow forever. It comes from a field of mathematical research called 'cellular automata' in which rules are applied to cells and their neighbours in a regular grid. It is a simple example of 'emergent complexity' or 'self-organizing systems' described in Chapter One and shows how elaborate patterns and behaviours can emerge from extremely simple rules. As such it has helped scientists and mathematicians understand such diverse effects as how the petals on a rose, or the stripes on a zebra can arise from a tissue of living cells growing alongside each other. It also helps explain the multiplicity of life that has evolved on earth. Indeed, scientists and mathematicians have now discovered that diversity is essential to life on this blue planet.

The Game of Life/complexity theory can be applied to families. Each of us belongs to clusters or structures we call families. These clusters or structures form patterns which maintain a particular stability and equilibrium by each member playing a specific role. This gives rise to a paradox: we want to maintain the closeness established in the family unit when we were children, but each of us is a developing human being reaching for our own independence and empowerment as we move from childhood to adulthood.

The way we attain this independence and empowerment is through change, but the unspoken dictates of families is to stay the same, for if we alter our unconsciously-designated role in the family, and change our patterns of silence or vagueness or blaming or anger or however that role has been shaped for us, we will automatically be met with strong opposition and a refusal by members of the family to accept it. Harriet Lerner called this a 'Change back!' reaction.[2] It is an explosive situation in which to find ourselves. Lerner maintained that in order for us to make changes within a family, we had to make them slowly, in small steps, so that there was time to observe and test their impact. If too much was changed too fast, it stirred up anxiety and emotional intensity and either old patterns and behaviours from the past were unconsciously re-imposed, or the person bringing in the change was expelled from the family unit. The Game of Life gave an understanding of the spectrum of difference that naturally occurs within families. My interviewees often observed how different they were from their siblings or parents, cousins, nephews or nieces. We accept variegation when it comes to flowers, dogs, cats and birds, yet somehow feel guilty when we see it in families. A family can therefore be defined as a subgroup in which each member sustains and supports a particular role in order to maintain the equilibrium.

When someone in the family dies, all the dynamics transform. A person in grief is not only dealing with the loss of their relationship to that individual, but also the ripples of metamorphosis that are caused by the death. All positions shift to fill the gap and there are conscious and unconscious bids for rank and jockeying for position. Changes are needed to allow the family to resettle into a position of safety. Nevertheless, under the stress of the situation and without external support, often these changes take place too quickly and cut-offs and splits in families occur. The Game of Life shows this as a naturally occurring pattern: members peel away from the main branch and begin a new sequence elsewhere. We may never know exactly why this is so and there is no blame in this. The one thing we do know is that this is the pattern of families.

Life expectancy
A hundred years ago, infant mortality was the expectation. It was common practice for a woman to bear many children, as it was a given that many would not live to full maturity. A walk through the cemeteries of the eighteenth- and nineteenth- centuries reveals a large percentage of graves of the very young. Prior to the emergence of twentieth century improvements in sanitation and living standards, children had a high death rate in their first seven years of life. The most life-threatening diseases were measles, scarlet fever, diphtheria and whooping cough, along with the more common pneumonia and diarrhoea. These have been the greatest threats to children throughout history and are still threats in developing countries. Whilst these infections now only account for about one percent of children's deaths in today's western world, medicine continues to be vigilant, as exemplified by a sign common in doctors' surgeries: 'Childhood diseases haven't died. Children have.'

Studies show it is normal for a child to experience a raft of diseases in the first seven years of life in order to strengthen their immune system.[3] Nevertheless, in the last fifty years we have grown so accustomed to western medicine finding solutions that we are shocked and horrified when deaths occur in childhood or adolescence. An ancient Chinese saying highlights this: 'The grandmother dies, the mother dies, the daughter dies.' This is the natural order of life and when that order is changed, it causes undercurrents for years to come. Many scholars consider that Constance's lines in *The Life and Death of King John* reflected Shakespeare's grief at the death of his son Hamnet in August, 1596 and thus identify the play as being written in that year:

Constance: Grief fills the room up of my absent child,
            Lies in his bed, walks up and down with me,
            Puts on his pretty looks, repeats his words,
            Remembers me of all his gracious parts,
            Stuffs out his vacant garments with his form.[4]

A story from the Buddhist tradition tells of Krishna Gotami, whose only son had died. Devastated, she carried her son to the Buddha and begged for a medicine that would bring him back to life. The Buddha nodded. It was indeed within his power to fulfil this wish, but first he must have a handful of mustard seeds. Krishna Gotami was overjoyed and immediately made plans to leave. The Buddha raised his hand. There was one proviso: each mustard seed had to come from a house where no-one had lost a child, a husband, a parent or a friend. After a long day of fruitless searching, pleading and, finally, despair, Krishna Gotami understood at last that birth and death are the opposite sides of the same coin. They cannot exist without each other and both are dependent upon each other to make the other real. She buried her son and returned to the Buddha to gain further wisdom from his teachings.

Jack - A Father in Grief

Although I have woven this account as a narrative, Jack told me the story of his son, Benjamin, as he remembered it — at times slowly and painfully, at other times stoically. At all times it was the song of a father in love.

The tapestry

When Benjamin was born on 29 May, 1973, in London, England, Jack (aged thirty-one and a half) already had two daughters. With enthusiastic Jewish aplomb, his aunts flourished a ring and a thread and came to the decisive conclusion that this child, too, was going to be a girl. Jack thought no more of it until the time of delivery when the doctor, who was a great soccer fan, exclaimed, 'Oh he's a big boy. He'll be a midfielder for Manchester United for sure!' Jack's knees buckled beneath him. He struggled for the door, certain he was going to faint. This was the son who would carry on the family name. The family business that had been passed on to Jack would now be passed on to Benjamin, the boy with the cheeky smile, the infectious laugh and the quick grin, for these, Jack felt, were the right qualities for the next caretaker of such a prestigious commerce. It was, however, more than this which drew Jack to his son. Benjamin was a great mimic and constantly had people in fits of laughter, quite often at his own expense. This meant that Benjamin was vulnerable and it was this quality of openness and receptivity that Jack loved most of all. 'I hug him often,' Jack wrote in his diary. 'I want him to know that he is so incredibly special to me. We laugh, we play pranks. He is the most beautiful boy I have ever seen. His beauty is much deeper than just the physical. We do so many things which we take for granted. Can father and son have a spiritual umbilical cord?'

In January 1992, Benjamin was eighteen years old, a six foot three inch athlete with the most engaging smile in the world. He was an extremely good tennis player, had already won several major tournaments on the ITF Junior Circuit and had been competing at Junior Wimbledon since he was fifteen. It was Jack's opinion that Benjamin could become a Wimbledon champion, but one thing bothered his coach. He could not understand why, with all his latent skill, lately Benjamin had stopped playing to his full potential. One moment he would be challenging with brilliant shots, a moment later he would be fumbling and groping at the ball as if it was beyond him to play the shot at all.

Benjamin also began acting erratically, jumping up and down on the spot in the kitchen as if limbering up on the tennis court. When Jack questioned this behaviour Benjamin looked at him curiously. 'What behaviour, Dad?' With Benjamin's GCSE A levels looming and pressure mounting, the doctor attributed it to stress before exams, and indeed when Benjamin received his final results, he found he had failed his A levels by one point. Jack was dissatisfied and he and his wife, Val, decided it was time for Benjamin to see a neurologist. The neurologist also connected this fluctuating behaviour with stress, yet MRI tests revealed a tumour on the right side of Benjamin's head. There was uncertainty about the cause, but it appeared to have been there for about six or seven years. The doctors reassured Jack and Val that it was readily removed by an operation and radiotherapy and this is what came to pass. Benjamin ended up with a scar across his forehead but recovered satisfactorily from the operation and with Val being the major breadwinner at that time in their lives, Jack was able to spend every day of the next few months with him.

Benjamin returned to the tennis court and within months, looking the embodiment of health, he began playing competition tennis. He and his girlfriend, Jenny, were a striking pair, soul mates sharing countless moments of happiness. Jack could see how much Jenny meant to Benjamin, how he was maturing and how all his tennis pupils adored him and he felt immense pride and happiness for 'his boy'. One night Benjamin sat down with his parents and told them he wanted to get back onto the European circuit to advance his ranking. Jack and Val looked at each other. Both of them knew this was an important step for Benjamin to truly develop the raw talent they saw in him, but he was still on specialised medication and they were reluctant to let him travel on his own. Tennis life was hard, Jack argued. You could end up sleeping anywhere: in a garage, in a pig-sty, on hay with the animals in a barn. Benjamin agreed. He knew the situation. He also knew that, given his age and recent history, it was now or never for him to make a serious bid at professional tennis. Neither Jack nor Val wanted to stop him from achieving his ambition, so they agreed to let him go.

Benjamin packed his bags and booked a flight to France. As the tapestry of his life became woven with French verbs and grammar, so his tennis, hewn and polished with regular challenge, became fluent on the court. In those days before the Internet he spoke with his parents often by telephone. During one such conversation, Jack realized Benjamin was slurring his words. Hesitantly he asked if he was okay. 'I have a headache', was Benjamin's reply. 'Are you taking your tablets?' Jack continued. Benjamin couldn't tell him. Jack's response was immediate. He asked the French family with whom Benjamin was lodging to take him to hospital. The hospital ran tests and found the tumour was back, and growing at an alarming rate. Jack arranged for a doctor to fly Benjamin back to London and a recommended surgeon operated with laser. In the aftermath of surgery they waited for the results. The surgeon arrived surrounded by his entourage. Brutally and without compassion he told them Benjamin didn't have long to live. Outraged, Jack and Val flew Benjamin to Edinburgh to a doctor who used thermal heat treatment against cancer cells. The intervention helped, but time was against them. Benjamin's brain began to swell and for several days he lay in a coma. Specialists advised them to take him off the life support system and, heavy of heart, they concurred. The green lines faded, but Benjamin's soul clung on. His mother and sister visited him and quietly offered their goodbyes. Then Jack was alone with his son, in the austere privacy of a sterile hospital room, facing the moment all parents dread and none believe will ever happen to them: the child of his loins untimely ripped from the net of life and time. In a sandpaper voice he told Benjamin how proud he was of him and what a wonderful son he had been. As the toll of minutes passed he knew he was to be Benjamin's Gate Keeper. 'Now,' he whispered. 'Now it is time for you to relax and let go.' He joined Val waiting patiently outside the room and in silence they found their way home. A few hours later the phone rang. Benjamin had died. It was 24 November 1992 and Benjamin was nineteen years old.

1993: The First Year

'Suddenly we are childless. The new and total silence in our lives is unbroken.' This quote from The Compassionate Friends website in 2003 sums up the stark and terrifying reality that floods many parents faced with the death of their child.[5] Jack and Val flew Benjamin's body back to London and both of them underwent a short period of grief counselling. Benjamin's death, however, had changed the family dynamics totally. Where previously the family had felt balanced with Jack, Val, their two daughters and Benjamin, Jack now felt completely swamped with female energy. He and Benjamin had shared common interests, cemented with a special bond of understanding. Jack described it as 'losing my best friend, the source of my joy, the comedian in the family.' Chaos and disorganisation now descended upon his life, the black melancholy of grief, and the recognition that life had eroded all that was important. He was being asked to lie down with the seals.

Isolation

The death of a child creates an unforeseen stress in marriages. There is a Jewish saying: 'Love is like bread, it must be made new each day.' All intimate relationships require this constant vigilance, yet when a child dies, not only will each partner express their distress differently, but grief is exhausting and will often take the form of withdrawal, leaving little room for either partner to attend to the other's needs. Some parents, heavy with torment and the onward echo of endless time, even consider taking their own lives in order to end their suffering and be reunited with their dead child. After Benjamin's death, Jack isolated himself. He went away on his own and he read books on grief, but

felt that nothing could help him understand the vale of
sorrow into which he had been plunged. He became religious and attended Orthodox Jewish services, but on the
Day of Atonement the words of the liturgy only inflamed
him. How could God decide who would live and who
would die? What right had God to take on that mantle of
omnipotence? Jack had felt good about being able to pass
on to Benjamin the values he had learned in life. They did
'boy' things together and Benjamin listened to him. One
day when Jack had walked Jenny home after services, she
had told him how proudly Benjamin had talked about the
things Jack had taught him, the small courtesies of life,
such as when being introduced to someone, how important it was to shake their hand firmly, look them in the
eye and call them by their name. Now there was no-one
to teach:

> No more fond admiration or encouraging words of
> praise
> 'That's awesome Dad! You're a champ!'
> Now only memories to cherish for a lifetime
> filled with infinite images of those dreams of what
> might have been.[6]

Jack did not sleep well and he developed acute headaches.
He dealt with Benjamin's death by writing him letters and
poems:

> ...My son, my most precious promise of tomorrow...
> I feel so alone.
> Who will now look up to me, who will ever compli-
> ment me,
> who will admire me ...
> who will need me that way ever again?

Parents who lose a child

As part of the grieving process, Jack and Val joined a group for parents who had lost children, but it didn't really achieve what Jack wanted. While he was there, he was told that the statistics of parents who break up after a child dies are exceedingly high. This frequently-quoted fact ranges anywhere from between fifty-to-eighty percent. In 1998, in an effort to discover the source of these statistics, Reiko Schwab conducted a review of the literature looking for such evidence.[7] She found no verification whatsoever in holding the death of a child liable for this high rate of divorce, nor did she find that the rate of divorce among bereaved parents was any higher than that of the general population. If marital stress was part of the relationship prior to the child's death, then the death made it evident that there was no longer any reason to solve the problems of a relationship that was no longer viable, and resulted in divorce. Those couples, however, whose relationships were well-established with ways of solving disagreements and differences of opinion prior to their child's death were more likely to continue the everyday spadework necessary to finding solutions, and hence kept their relationships intact. In the same way as a person may feel anger at the circumstances surrounding a death, so it is possible that the rate of divorce may be affected by the circumstances of death, for example, if one of the parents believed the other parent contributed to the child's demise. Thus statistics such as those quoted above, passed on by professionals who omitted to examine the cited sources and who then used them to predict a likely outcome, are somewhat alarming. They add an unwarranted layer of anxiety onto the shoulders of bereaved parents who may be concerned that their marriage won't survive the loss. Schwab's research showed that the majority of marital relationships not only outlast the severe demands on the marriage brought about by a child's death, but may even be strengthened by it in the long run.

Jack was aware that Benjamin had been his ally. When he turned to Val, he felt only her distance and detachment. Val had never really been able to talk about deep, personal issues and now, more than anything else, Jack wanted honesty. If he couldn't have a close relationship with his wife, then what was the point in them being together. Faced with his own mortality, feeling time to be at its most potent now, he understood, in a space deep within him, that for however long the rest of his life promised to be, he wanted quality in those remaining years. With Benjamin gone and Val unreachable and withdrawn, Jack hated coming home. With a shock, he realised that their marriage had been a shell held together for the sake of the children. Six months after Benjamin died, Jack and Val separated.

For most of 1993 Jack attended personal growth groups. They were not necessarily connected with grieving, but were groups which helped Jack express his feelings: one was on intimacy; another was on breath work, encouraging people to release emotions through exhalation. It was in these groups that Jack began to realise that many people carry pain and for quite different reasons. From the space of 'I am the one suffering and feeling sorry for myself', he became empathic, open and able to talk about what happened, an expression of the new growth and learning that was entering his life.

Dreaming of Benjamin

At that point Jack began to dream of Benjamin. His initial response on waking was distress, knowing that time in the dream with Benjamin was limited due to his illness. Jack's words were: 'There is always the concern, the fear, the sorrow of knowing. It's never a dream like a normal dream. There is always the component of knowing that he's going to be here for just awhile and then he's going to be gone.' Even when Jack dreamed that Benjamin was fully recovered, there was pressure to appreciate the moment and enjoy what was happening. It wasn't until he became aware of how much joy he gained by being with Benjamin in his dreams that he really began to look forward to them. Meanwhile he was experiencing a long and drawn out divorce with Val. Jack had always said he would split everything fifty-fifty with Val, even the family business, which had been passed on to him by his father. Val and her advisers valued the business unrealistically, however, and she became bitter, suspicious and extremely antagonistic towards Jack. It took two years for the divorce to be settled.

Jack's social patterns also took a surprising turn. In March, 1993, Jack met Carol at one of his personal growth groups. It was a time when people who had completed such workshops would give each other a hug if they met again socially, something that never used to happen. At a wedding a short time later, the last function Jack attended with Val, he re-encountered Carol and she threw her arms around him. As he hugged her back, Jack felt a spark between them. Only four months since Benjamin's death, getting involved in a relationship was the last thing he wanted. By now, however, insomnia was wracking his body and as Carol was a body worker who specialised in releasing emotional blocks held in the muscles, Jack decided to see her professionally. After one session, Jack slept soundly for the first time in months. When Jack separated from Val, he and Carol started seeing each other as friends, but Jack found himself in emotional turmoil: he was not ready to get involved in a relationship and yet he enjoyed her company, so they decided to keep meeting and talking, but did not go out together socially.

Family undercurrents

As always, a change in one part of a family causes changes elsewhere. His younger daughter, Kathy, asked Jack if he thought he would ever remarry. He said he wouldn't. In December, 1993, however, when Jack had been on his own for six months, he told his older daughter, Amanda, that he was starting to see somebody. 'That's a bit sudden, isn't it?' was her immediate response. Jack was taken aback and yet he could understand her reaction. Amanda was Val's daughter from her first marriage and she had experienced the marriage break-up at the age of four. Now the same event was happening all over again. Jack trod carefully. Yes, it was sudden, he said, but he had no intention of getting seriously involved. He really liked Carol and he would probably start going out with her. From that moment on Amanda stopped speaking to Jack. Jack tried several times to re-establish a relationship with Amanda but each time was unsuccessful. To add to his pain, Amanda's son, Jack's first grandchild, had been born the day after Benjamin died. To Jack it seemed that everything had a price. Not only had he lost a son, now he had also lost a daughter and a grandson as well. Jack's grip on Proteus tightened.

1994: The Second Year — Disorganisation

In 1994 Jack began working as a healer and a counsellor in earnest. He specialised in massage and esoteric healing and he tailor-made audio meditation tapes to help his clients with specific areas of concern in their life. He found he was extremely good at this work. He was developing his ability to understand and share the feelings of another. Sensitive and open about her emotions, Carol formed a stark contrast to Val. It was in this year that they began courting each other seriously. Carol wanted to get married; Jack felt it was too soon. Two years after his son's death, he was still in a state of disorganisation.

1995: The Third Year — Navigation

Jack's and Val's divorce became legal in June 1995. Jack and Carol travelled overseas to attend an advanced course in esoteric healing and it was here they became engaged. In December 1995, they were married. Proteus was now vanquished and had given Jack the answers he was seeking: he had successfully reached the safety of the shores of home — and home lay with Carol.

1996: The Fourth Year — Joy and expansion

1996 was dominated by expansion, change, and an enriched existence. Jack's life was underscored by a happiness and joy he had been craving as the underpinning to his life: a partner with whom he could communicate freely and take joy in their daily routines together. Jack was ready to reach outwards in his world, now that the new roots he was putting down were starting to take hold. Nearly four years after Benjamin's death, Jack continued to process the grief. Counsellors said he held deep-seated anger, but Jack didn't feel that was the case. He never felt that there was anger and, as noted earlier, anger doesn't have to be part of the grieving process. Always aware of his shortcomings as well as his strengths and now defining himself as more intuitively aware, Jack felt he had a good grasp on what was going on inside himself. There was pain and sorrow and the difficulty of understanding why, but never anger.

There were moments when memory overtook him and the emotions surfaced, as deep and profound as when Benjamin first died. 'Sometimes weeks can go by and you think that you've come to terms with it, but every now and then something happens and it just reaches right deep within you and you know that you'll always have that deep, deep pain.' This sorrow for Benjamin contained a far different quality to the grief he felt when his father died. Jack now came to understand that loss held many flowers in its bouquet, and the death of a parent was what was expected in time. Through Benjamin's death, however, Jack had experienced a unique pain that allowed him to become much more accepting and far less judgemental of other people.

1997: The Fifth Year — Metamorphosis

1997 was the fifth year after Benjamin's death. For some years Jack had neither ambition nor drive. He would 'just get by day by day'. Now he looked outward for new challenges and cherished his social networks for the new ideas they fed him. This was the year Jack took over as Chairman of the business in London and committed to it in a whole new way.

And after...

From the year of worry and concern prior to Benjamin's death through the grinding abrasion of the five years following it, in 1998-1999 it was as if, rather than having to face external pressures, Jack now had 'time off' to assess his place in life. Indeed, Jack described the last few months of 1999 as bringing with it a sense of re-emergence in the business with him having more of a corporate profile.

In 2000, Jack and Carol bought a large country property in Gloucestershire with various farming activities stimulating new challenges, new subjects to learn and further changes. Since Benjamin's death Jack had no longer considered himself to be religious. Now for the first time in seven years, he attended services. He described himself as less angry with God and more accepting that Judaism was his faith. He accepted what he could and also felt free to dismiss or reject what was not acceptable to him. Before Benjamin's death Jack characterized himself as being 'decidedly closed, a bit of a poker face'. Through the courses he attended, he learned to express his feelings and to become aware of other people's torment, allowing him to see life from a quite different perspective.

Jack doesn't go to the cemetery much now because, he says, 'Benjamin's not there.' Instead it is in his dreams where Benjamin is alive. Sometimes he is six or seven years old and Jack is teaching him to play tennis. Sometimes he is fully recovered and a teenager. Often no words are spoken. In whatever way the dreams manifest, they are always happy times. Jack wakes filled with Benjamin's love and joy and the happiness stays with him. In late 1999, on the anniversary of Benjamin's death, Jack offered to go with Val to the cemetery. Val declined. Her memory of Benjamin's death remained centred on that last week, the distress of his condition and his lifeless body. Despite years of happiness, some people only remember the person they loved in these last difficult moments, such as Jane's Aunt Deirdre who could not sleep for 'seeing Uncle Andrew collapsing in the doorway over and over.' This is a heavy load to bear for the rest of one's life.

The most difficult times for Jack were the first three years after Benjamin's death, which swept away the last vestiges of a life in which he had hermetically sealed his feelings. Benjamin's death was a lever on the lid of Jack's emotions and like a cyclone they rushed in to fill the gap of loss. As this life at sea settled to a steady rhythm, Jack found himself breathing new air. What he learnt from Benjamin's death now formed the foundation for the rest of his life.

Hannah - A Mother In Grief

Hannah's interview in 1999 emerged in a slightly different way. She had sought my opinion on whether she should reconnect with a man from her past when her story of unresolved grief gushed out. I asked if we could change the parameters to a more formal semi-structured interview. Although cautious and concerned that her identity not be revealed in any way, she agreed. This is what emerged.

Hannah's history of loss had begun at age five, when she and her family moved from the city to the country, leaving behind all her friends. At age ten her friend was killed by a car (February), her cat died (November) and so did her paternal grandmother (December). Then at age eleven, she experienced a loss of innocence and trust through being sexually abused by her friend's father at her friend's birthday party. Already many templates of how to deal — or not deal — with loss had taken hold and were deeply rooted in her psyche. The narrative she revealed, however, was pattern-rich and as she moved more deeply into the telling, so her breathing relaxed and her face lightened. Here is her story.

The story begins...

In 1971, when Hannah was nearly sixteen, her maternal grandfather — 'the one person in my life who seemed to love me unconditionally' — fell ill. Knowing he was dying and believing he would not see Christmas, he asked Hannah to come down on the train from the country and visit him in the city where he lived. Hannah's parents did not take his request seriously and refused her permission to go. On Christmas Eve her grandfather collapsed on the bathroom floor from an embolism, fell against the door, and died at five minutes to midnight. Her grandmother couldn't move him out of the bathroom and that was also the night the ambulances had chosen to go on strike. Hannah said:

> I believed for years that, had I gone down, I could
> have helped. I felt I had let him down. I took the
> phone call in the evening about him dying but
> my father wouldn't let me tell the other kids until
> after Christmas Day. I remember that day being
> the longest of my life —and I ran away from home
> that afternoon. No one really helped me through
> it. No-one helped me with my grief. My father is
> uncomfortable about expressing emotions and I make

him uncomfortable because I have always been the
opposite. No-one seemed to notice anything. After
Pop died, my Grandmother became an incurable
alcoholic. No-one dealt with or addressed that, either.
I felt terribly abandoned and terribly alone, cut off
from people and not part of the world.

Hannah's way of coping was through isolating herself,
through reading books, walking and being on her own.

In 1975, when Hannah was nineteen and by then a
gifted violinist, a friend asked her to record a couple of
tracks with a guitarist. When she arrived at her friend's
place, she was introduced to Art, the young man playing
guitar. They fell desperately in love, but her father did not
approve of the relationship and when he told Hannah
she had to make a choice, she felt it was an easy one to
make. She left home with Art the next day and not long
afterwards they married. Despite mixed feelings about her
parents, Hannah felt a great sense of loss and sadness, but
time had to pass before she was ready to see them again.
In 1982, seven years after they married, when Hannah
was twenty-six, there were clearly unresolved issues in the
relationship. As the worries came to a crescendo, she and
Art split up and Hannah fell head over heels in love with
Sean, a man with whom she played music and who had
been married but was now separated. During the time of
his affair with Hannah, Sean vacillated between staying
with her and going back to his wife. Fed up with being
the patsy, Hannah forced his hand. She removed herself
from the situation, in effect making the decision for him,
and Sean went back to his wife. On the rebound, feeling
miserable and unloved, Hannah briefly became involved

with someone else and fell pregnant. At six weeks she made the decision to have a termination. The operation proceeded without a hitch and two weeks later she returned to have an IUD inserted.

Some weeks passed and she felt really off-colour. She rang her doctor and told him that she still felt sick, that in her opinion she didn't think she had recovered from the operation and furthermore, she didn't understand why she was feeling like this. The doctor told her it had been a difficult time, that it was logical she would feel this way and not to worry, that things would get better in a few more weeks. A few more weeks passed and she didn't feel any better. Now deeply concerned, she made another doctor's appointment. 'Look,' she asserted, 'I've got all the symptoms of pregnancy. I still feel pregnant'. Her doctor replied: 'You can't be!' He carried out some tests and sent Hannah to have some scans, which she was given in a packet without explanation. A good deal more frightened and placid than she was now, she did not ask what they revealed. Instead she returned them to her doctor who informed her that she was seventeen weeks pregnant. There had been a twin pregnancy. They had removed one of the embryos and not the other.

Hannah was appalled that this could have happened, particularly with the insertion of the IUD. The doctor defended himself by saying that, since they weren't expecting anything, they didn't know to look for it. To them it appeared to be a swelling from the operation. Hannah had two options: to go ahead with the pregnancy or to have a mid-trimester termination. Hannah wanted neither. She was completing her Diploma in Education (Dip.Ed.), she was not in a relationship, she already had two little girls from her marriage to Art, and she had no money. She had arranged her life so she could start teaching by the end of that year with the aim of earning a decent enough income to give her young girls what she thought they needed. She was also pulled by the little soul growing inside her.

She decided to go ahead and have the baby, but the underlying feeling was shame. It wasn't Art's baby which would, in some way, have legitimised the pregnancy and it wasn't Sean's baby, the person she had really wanted as the father. At the end of the day, it was a mistake. She didn't really want it and what was more relevant, she didn't want other people to know about it, so she hid it. In those days it was an easy thing for her to do. She knew from both her previous pregnancies that she never showed much until about seven months, so when she did, she wore baggy jumpers. She managed to avoid running into Art, who had access to the children every second weekend, by letting him collect them directly from child care. This arrangement suited them both since they were still intensely angry with each other.

When Hannah was just under eight months pregnant, she felt the world become exceptionally quiet, free from ripples or splintered time. She thought nothing of it, went to bed and slept through the whole night. As she prepared for bed the next evening, she realised what was wrong. The reason she had been able to sleep was because she hadn't been disturbed. In pregnancy both her other two children had woken her around three in the morning by kicking and this one was no different. This night, however, there was nothing, no movement, no activity, only stillness. The next day in surgery the doctor couldn't pick up a heartbeat and tests on her amniotic fluid showed that the baby had died somewhere in the previous twenty-four to thirty-six hours. Hannah described her response as 'incredible guilt'. She said, 'It was obviously something that I had willed. I didn't want it and so therefore I was going to make damn sure I didn't have it one way or the other.' The next step was to induce the baby before the placenta began to decay. Her previous children had been easy deliveries, birthed quickly without delay: Lizzie, her eldest daughter, born sixteen minutes after Hannah went in to hospital; Stella, her second daughter, born after forty-six minutes of labour. This induction took twenty-seven hours, a total shock to Hannah, but then part of her felt that this was not a birth. This was something different and Hannah was hanging on, not wanting to let go, not wanting to face events. Hannah described the birth as 'dreamy, surreal. I wasn't conscious. I went into some kind of respiratory —... not failure but I remember being extremely light-headed and losing consciousness.' In reality it was a type of shock connected with her heart and respiration. Hannah had an irregular heart beat which only surfaced in times of severe stress, and labour is the most stressful event a woman can experience. The same reaction had occurred during both her daughters' births, but since they were uncommonly quick, it hadn't been a serious issue. Hannah had spoken to the doctor about this after the first birth and his reply was that if this only happened when Hannah was in severe stress, then it wasn't something with which she need concern herself on a daily level. Inducing this baby turned into a long and protracted process, however, and although it wasn't a matter of life and death, Hannah passed out. When her body had been stabilised and she had regained consciousness, the baby was gone.

Hannah's rights as a mother

This action raises interesting questions around the rights of the hospital to remove the baby's body without the mother's permission. Despite what Hannah felt about the way it was conceived, when a woman has carried a child nearly full term and built a relationship with the soul growing inside her, such an action of removal was never going to be the resolution to losing this significant relationship. One of the women who answered my grief questionnaire had a miscarriage at the age of thirty-five. Ten years later, in the year 2000, this was how she remembered it:

> Miscarriage at twelve weeks. A voice in my head telling me I had to let go, that this child was not meant to be. Insisting that I be taken to hospital, even though there were no strong physical signs of a miscarriage. Calmness and a sense of dissociation when the miscarriage happened after a day in hospital. Sensation of coldness, emptiness, numbness, total removal of the senses. The next day physical after-effects, like I had been kicked in the stomach. Rawness, like physical pain but not physical. Nausea, bitter taste, blackness. I can remember these things. And then crying — I am not a cryer by nature — crying and crying and crying like never before. Totally untouchable — no-one could get near me. Rage and then emptiness. Depression. Removal from everyone — loss of direction, difficult, prickly, inconsolable, exhausted.

The length of a pregnancy is not a measure of the depth of grief. Sands, the miscarriage, stillbirth, and neonatal death charity in the UK, noted that while the rate of stillbirths has diminished since 2011 as a result of advances in medical knowledge and clinical care 'in the UK in 2015, one in every 227 births was a stillbirth, and there were 3,434 stillbirths in total. That's around nine babies stillborn every day'.[8] Sands Australia estimates that 'one in four pregnancies (93,000) ends in miscarriage in Australia each year, while approximately 2,500 babies are either stillborn or die in the first 28 days after birth.'[9] The website adds the devastating statement that 'Despite the fact that the death of a baby affects so many Australians, it remains a topic that is rarely spoken about in public.' Spending time with the stillborn baby, seeing the body, naming it, and taking photographs is now considered a healthy way of dealing with the grief. These small gestures allow the development of memories and provide a focus for the parents' feelings. No matter how painful, these simple acts provide the reality and context to enable a person to grieve. It didn't occur to Hannah to assert her rights and ask for her baby, so she didn't see the body and she had no idea what had happened to it once it was delivered. She didn't know how to deal with her feelings and, since Art was not around to help, her overriding motivation was to stay strong for her girls.

With her Dip.Ed. safely in place, Hannah rang the Education Department two days before placements went out: 'Send me to the outback. I'll go anywhere.' In December, Hannah left the city with her two little girls and severed all connections with anyone she knew. In outback Australia she made an abundance of new friends who did not know her and did not know her history. She, however, thought about it all the time and she felt a terrible guilt that somehow *She Had Done It*. With no outlet for the expression of her pain, it became jammed in her unconscious and a deep depression set in for roughly seven years. Like Menelaus, Hannah was captain of a ship going nowhere.

In this first year of her grief, a year of quietness and slow, inward processing would have helped Hannah immensely. In a state of confusion and disintegration, without major external events jostling for position in her life, Hannah could then have given herself a chance to integrate the loss and make adjustments to her life. This was, however, suppressed grief and none of this happened. Instead in 1984 Hannah experienced excessive trauma and crisis when her house in the city, which she had rented out, was trashed so badly she had to sell it. In 1985 she began a new, intense, intimate relationship which polarised her friends, some of whom she lost as a result. In 1986 Hannah fell off her verandah and shattered her elbow so badly that she lost the use of her right arm for four months. A plate was inserted which stayed in her arm for seven years until the bones knitted:

> I also injured my back and was in physiotherapy for a long time. I lost a great deal of mobility including the ability to play my violin, to swing a golf club or to lift a tennis racquet. I couldn't play netball anymore because I was afraid of falling over. I also lost a lot of money in medical bills until some compensation money, just enough to cover the bills, came through five years later.

Fourteen years after her baby died
When Hannah was forty, she moved back to the city. Once again she was in a relationship with someone that she cared about greatly. Once again she found out she was pregnant. This time she felt as if she had been hit over the head with a hammer. She couldn't see this relationship being perma-

nent and she didn't want to go through another pregnancy alone a second time. Once again she decided to terminate the pregnancy. Some weeks later she still felt really off-colour. This time she knew. She went back and had a second termination two weeks later. Her past experience had given her the insight to understand the physical nature of what was happening and she was correct, it was a twin. The same thing had happened again.

Hannah's paternal grandmother had been a faith healer, detached and slightly other-worldly in many ways, yet always kind. She had half-terrified and half-amazed Hannah, who was nearly eleven when her grandmother died. Hannah missed her greatly and wished she had been able to see more of her. As a child Hannah had thought faith healing so odd she had ignored, it but when the same pattern of pregnancy surfaced, she went to see a clairvoyant. This was the first time in fourteen years that Hannah had talked to anyone about what had happened. The woman told her it wasn't her fault, that it was the child who had changed her mind, that this little soul trying to come through was born into the wrong generation and it wasn't meant to be like this.

Hannah didn't believe her. She thought it was a really convenient psychological model that people could believe if they wanted, but in her case it didn't work like that. A few nights later Hannah saw her mother. She said nothing about going to see the clairvoyant, nor anything of what she had been told. Of her own volition her mother told her that when she was first married she had fallen pregnant, and the baby had died in the womb. Some months later, feeling most unwell, her mother had gone to see the doctor. The doctors were of the opinion that Hannah's mother could not possibly still be pregnant, but she was — with Hannah. Hannah was one of a twin. The other twin had died in the womb. Not only that, but her grandmother and her great-grandmother had also lost babies. Four generations of women had a repeating pattern of infant loss.

Hannah realised that her emotional wellbeing was intimately tied up with this inherited family pattern of the lost twin, reverberating like an echo through the generations, a pattern looped in time trying to resolve itself. Hannah was nineteen when she married. Seven years later she was divorced. Fourteen years passed between the first aborted twin pregnancy and the second one. Hannah was clearly responding to a seven-year cyclic pattern. Now she was piecing together another pattern — a puzzle that involved four generations of the women of her family and a pattern of twins. Suddenly this answered a whole lot of questions for her. She had always felt like she had no clear identity, no lucid memories of childhood or adolescence: 'Like, it didn't happen. I can't put borders around it.' When Hannah found out she was pregnant again, all the old emotions resurfaced: 'It wasn't like this event had nothing to do with anything else. It's not in little bits. It all flies back in.' This was unresolved grief as potent and powerful as it had originally expressed itself. So Hannah began talking to her unborn daughter at night, letting her know that again the time was wrong. Communicating in this way, consciously acknowledging the history of which she recognized she was now an important part, Hannah began to feel her own twin around her less and less.

Lone twins

Joan Woodward, a psychotherapist working in Birmingham, England, lost her identical twin sister from meningitis at the age of three. Since then she had become acutely aware of having distinctly different feelings from her singleton friends. In order to understand this further, between 1983 and 1986 she interviewed 219 volunteer lone twins, both men and women, in England and Wales, ranging in age from eighteen to ninety-two. Some had lost their twin at or around birth, some in childhood and others in adult life. Ninety of them were identical (monozygots), one hundred and eleven were fraternal (dizygots) and eighteen did not know their zygosity. Eighty-one percent of the lone twins interviewed described their loss as having either a severe or a marked effect on their lives, the severest felt by those who had lost a twin of the same sex, whether identical or not, and those who had lost their twin before the age of six months. Woodward believed this was due to the fact that their experience of loss was at a preverbal age when they were unable to express what they were feeling, and separation anxiety became locked in to the behaviour sequence, giving rise to such symptoms as depression, fear, feelings of inadequacy, extreme anger, and violence. In addition, the surviving twin not only had to cope with their own feelings, but with their parents' emotional anguish as well.

No research work at all had been carried out in this field until Woodward's study, which was presented at the 1988 International Conference of Twin Studies in Amsterdam and published in the Journal of their Proceedings a year later, then as a book.[10] The most controversial part of this study was the area that focused on twin loss in the womb or at birth. Most psychiatrists and psychoanalysts doubted whether memories in the womb or at birth could contribute to the surviving twin's sense of loss. Attachment theorists believe attachment behaviour comes into being around six months of age. Woodward believed otherwise and cited the work of Alessandra Piontelli who, in 1992, observed the behaviour of twins in the womb via scans and discovered that the way twins related to each other in the womb was reflected in the way they related to each other as babies.[11] Piontelli's videos, Woodward argued, showed clear evidence that twins in the womb responded to each other and that the death of one of them and their subsequent removal from the womb had serious consequences for the remaining twin. Woodward's study confirmed that the loss of a twin, at whatever age, was a profound experience for the other twin, and left them feeling a relentless sense of incompleteness. Woodward reasoned that, possibly because twins were only noticed when they were seen together, such feelings were often diminished as invalid. This loss, however, was significant and needed to be endorsed and acknowledged as a crucial experience which affected the lone twin for its entire life.[12]

The case of Samuel Armas

In support of this idea are the somewhat controversial photographs taken during a revolutionary operation on 19 August, 1999, to fix the spina bifida lesion of a twenty-one-week-old foetus, Samuel Alexander Armas, in the womb.[13] Julie Armas, a twenty-seven year old obstetrics nurse in Atlanta, Georgia, USA, and her husband Alex, a twenty-eight year-old jet aircraft engineer, had been desperately trying to conceive a baby. Julie had previously suffered two miscarriages, so when, at fourteen weeks, she began to experience appalling cramps, she was given an ultrasound scan to observe the shape of the developing foetus and its position in the womb. The scan revealed that Samuel had a misshapen brain and that part of his spinal cord was exposed after the backbone failed to develop. He had spina bifida, a congenital neurological disorder marked by underdeveloped vertebrae that leave the spinal cord exposed. It occurs in about one in one thousand pregnancies. Though not always fatal, the most severe form, myelocele, involves a physical change in the spinal cord itself and can result in severe physical handicaps if the child survives and is untreated.

Julie and Alex were devastated. They were offered the routine, and perfectly legal, procedure of termination and many parents would have accepted. Julie and Alex were deeply religious, however, and it was not a course of action they wished to follow. Instead, Julie's mother found a website on the internet which detailed the pioneering surgery of neurologist Dr Joseph Bruner and his team at Vanderbilt University Hospital in Nashville, Tennessee. Although the results had not (then) been endorsed in medical journals, the surgical team had developed a technique for correcting foetal problems in mid-pregnancy by temporarily removing the uterus, draining the amniotic fluid, performing surgery on the tiny foetus entirely through a tiny slit in the wall of the womb, then restoring the uterus back inside the mother. The instruments had to be specially designed to work in miniature and the sutures used to close the incisions were less than the thickness of a human hair. Controversy surrounded surgery like this, because it opposed the general medical rule that risk should not outweigh benefit. Julie and Alex were fully aware that if anything went wrong, no attempt would be made to deliver Samuel by Caesarean section, since medical science did not yet have the capability of keeping a twenty-one-week old foetus alive outside the womb and that, as a safety precaution, a crash-cart would be on standby for Julie throughout the operation. Julie's response was clear: 'The worst thing might be if we don't do this and this is standard treatment when he's twenty-one years old, and he says: "Why didn't you know about that?" and we say, "We did, but we didn't do it for you."'[14]

Samuel Armas was the fifty-fourth foetus operated on by the surgical team and the entire surgical procedure was completed in one hour and thirteen minutes. Bruner says that both Samuel and Julie were under anaesthesia during the operation and could not move. Michael Clancy was the veteran photojournalist in Nashville, Tennessee, hired by *USA Today* newspaper to photograph the operation. This is what he saw:

> When it was over, the surgical team breathed a sigh of relief, as did I. As the doctor asked me what speed of film I was using, out of the corner of my eye I saw the uterus shake but no one's hands were near it. It was shaking from within. Suddenly, an entire arm thrust out of the opening, then pulled back until just a little hand was showing. The doctor reached over and lifted the hand, which reacted and squeezed the doctor's finger. As if testing for strength, the doctor shook the tiny fist. Samuel held firm. I took the picture! …
>
> It was ten days before I knew if the picture was even in focus. To ensure no digital manipulation of images before they see them, *USA Today* required that film be

submitted unprocessed. When the photo editor finally phoned me he said, 'It's the most incredible picture I've ever seen.'[15]

Bruner's account is that he saw the hand 'sort of pop up in the incision' from the womb and he 'reached over and picked it up.' Clancy shot a couple of frames and Bruner tucked the hand back into the womb. 'Why did I pick up the hand?' Bruner asked. 'I have no idea why I did it. I looked and I saw this hand and I guess that to me it was just a very human thing to do to reach out and shake somebody's hand.'

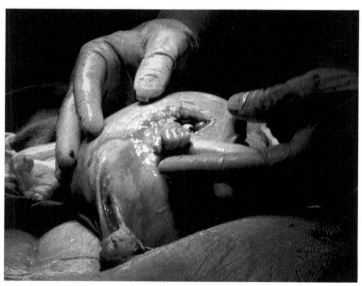

Reproduced with kind permission from the photojournalist © Michael Clancy, 1999.

The surgery was successful and Samuel was born at thirty-six weeks on 2 December 1999, at 6:25 pm at

Northside Hospital, weighing five pounds eleven ounces and measuring twenty-and-a-half inches long. He did not have to spend any time in a neonatal unit and an ultrasound showed he did not have any hydrocephalus and the brain malformation had resolved. He moved his legs well from the hips and had some movement from the knees. Although a frank breech (folded in half) in the womb, the orthopaedist was confident Samuel stood a good chance of walking. Whilst pro-life and religiously conservative groups have been quick to embrace Clancy's photographs as indications of the conscious action of a twenty-one-week-old foetus, Bruner maintained that both Samuel and his mother were anesthetised. Clancy's stance was simple: 'The picture is proof that at twenty-one weeks in utero, the child is a reactive human being and that anesthetising a foetus is the most experimental thing about this surgery.' Until further work is done in this field, it will always spark controversy. Nevertheless, reactive or conscious, life is clearly formed and functioning at this time. Its implication for a lone twin in the womb, in such a confined space, is both unsettling and profound.

Missing link

At what point in time parents tell the lone twin of the situation, how they tell them, and their attitude afterwards all play a vital role in the lone twin's acceptance of the loss. Most lone twins on hearing their story feel they have found a missing link. So it was with Hannah. Hannah said:

> I have this extremely social side that fills in all the gaps
> and people have this perception of me being such an
> open person and I'm not. I'm remarkably private. I

have this part of me that's totally intimidated by the
dark that's inside me and so only goes to this line and
no further. It's not that I do it deliberately. It's just that
I don't quite know how to get my tongue around the
words, like it won't come out. That's why I get all these
chest infections and can't breathe.

In 1998 Sean finally left his wife for good. Hannah had
been extremely angry with him over a whole range of issues
and didn't respond when he contacted her. Six months into
the year, his daughter, aged eighteen, crashed a car into
a tree and was killed instantly. This child was Hannah's
god-daughter, a child she had fed when a baby while Sean's
wife was ill and raised as one of her own in her first few
years of life. All Hannah's anger at Sean dissolved. All that
was on her mind was that Sean needed support, but his
daughter's death brought up immense guilt connected to
all her unresolved grief. Sean told Hannah that as soon as
she said the word, he would be there to form a committed
relationship with her. At the beginning of 1999, this was
the question on her mind: should she be with Sean or not?

Hannah was not ready for bereavement counselling
in 1982. She participated in a little after the termination
in 1996, but didn't feel it was useful because she still
felt ashamed and couldn't tell her whole story. When I
interviewed Hannah in 1999 this was the first time she
had ever told anyone the whole story. For the first time she
began to get a handle on the emergent patterns. There were
clear messages: it was time to deal with her unresolved grief
and it was time to be clear about her relationship with Sean.
Hannah knew Sean was desperate to replace his daughter.
She also knew that for her, another pregnancy was now

totally out of the question. Knowing she had to maintain her integrity and draw a clear line in the sand, once more she sent him packing.

Hannah started to re-establish links with the people she had known before her pregnancy in 1982 and, slowly and painfully, she started to speak out about her history. In mid-2000 she wrote to me:

> I have had what I regard as an extraordinarily rich and full life. Along with all these losses I feel quite blessed. I have an amazing network of loving friends, wonderful kids, a brain that seeks out and desires new things and that will never stay still and generally good health. I love my life and wouldn't want another. I would never make the same decisions now as I may have five years ago. I am a much stronger individual who is able to prioritise her own needs more effectively than before, although some of this still fails me from time to time. Those boundaries have been hard won, but I know my limits and I know the things that hook me into situations that I can do without. Even my relationship with my parents is much more grounded now, although I will probably never be close to them.
>
> My earliest memory is trying to get the sun out of my eyes. I remember not being able to do this. I must have only been a year or so, just a baby, and the dominant feeling was discomfort. Perhaps that's been a theme in my life that is now finally starting to change.
>
> My own involvement has prevented me from seeing the relationships between events and perhaps, truthfully, my hesitancy to deal with parts of my strange life. I want to thank you for helping me to do this. It made me reflect a lot at the time and I really

enjoyed working with you; your patience and care,
and sensitivity was immensely special.

The cycle in Hannah's life which began in 1972 offered
her as its prelude the death of her grandfather. Twenty-
seven years later, the encrusted layers were beginning to
dissolve, exposing the heart of the matter. In the myth of
grief Proteus had spoken and Hannah had found her voice.
She was now free to sail home to her changed world. Her
life was now made of a completely different texture and
fabric, although she was still respectful of the fact that the
past had a way of repeating itself with a twist. In October
2003, Hannah emailed me: 'Oh and by the way, I don't
know if I told you — Sean became a grandfather last year
and, you guessed it: twins.'

Conclusion

Grief is a long-term process and its function is to facilitate
the healing process by acknowledging what has occurred,
including any past patterns, and shifting it into a bigger
picture. Acknowledging all the memories that wove the
relationship together, the bitter and the sweet, enables the
past to become part of the person's present, making the
memories normal and putting them into the context of the
storyline of the person's life.

What anyone in grief is desperately seeking is a
benevolent heart and a stay of time, a place where the
world will not collapse in on them and a place where
they do not have to pretend. If grief has been suppressed,
what emerges in the safety and security of someone who
will listen is the sound of a broken heartstring as it tries
to keep playing the tune of life. Any offer of the space to

talk filled with empathy means the person can step forward with their life bearing the gift of their future. It may take many more months, perhaps years, of walking through the unique topography that is their grief and talking about it, but at least they will have understood there is a pathway to walk. If you have listened well enough, you will have shone a light onto their way through the woods, revealing that through the prickly branches and the mist, life awaits them at the edge of the forest, dressed in cloths of gold and sustained with love and warmth.

> The wind brings
> enough fallen leaves
> to make a fire.
>
> Ryokan (Japanese poet, 1758-1831)

Notes

1. http://mathworld.wolfram.com/GameofLife.html - accessed 25 March 2019

2. Harriet Goldhor Lerner, *The Dance of Anger: A Woman's Guide to Changing the Patterns of Intimate Relationships* (New York: Harper Collins, 1985), pp14-15.

3. Joseph Mercola, 'Do You Make This Common Mistake When Your Child Is Sick?', http://articles.mercola.com/sites/articles/archive/2011/02/03/the-benefits-of-fever.aspx - acccessed 21 November 2016.

4. William Shakespeare. 'King John' (3.4.93-97) in Stephen Greenblatt et al., eds. *The Norton Shakespeare*. New York: W.W. Norton & Company, Inc., 1997, p.1094.

5. The Compassionate Friends is a national non-profit, self-help support organization in both the UK and USA offering friendship and understanding to families grieving the death of a child of any age, from any cause. There is no religious

affiliation. https://www.tcf.org.uk/ and https://www.
compassionatefriends.org/

6.   My sincere thanks to Jack for allowing me to publish his
     poetry.

7.   Reiko Schwab, 'A Child's Death and Divorce: Dispelling the
     Myth', *Death Studies* 5 (1998), p.445.

8.   https://www.sands.org.uk/our-work/baby-death-current-
     picture/how-many-babies-die - accessed 7 February 2019

9.   http://www.sands.org.au/about-us - accessed 7 February
     2019.

10. Joan Woodward, *The Lone Twin: A Study in Bereavement
     and Loss* (London: Free Association Books, 1998).

11. Alessandra Piontelli, From *Fetus to Child: An Observational
     and Psychoanalytic Study* (London: Routledge, 1992),
     pp.235-236.

12. In May 1989 Woodward set up The Lone Twin Network
     (originally called the Lone Twin Register) to offer support to
     anyone who has experienced twin bereavement, at whatever
     stage of life. Based in the UK, the Network has members
     across the world: https://lonetwinnetwork.org.uk/

13. I am indebted to personal communication with Michael
     Clancy for information on this story. See also http://
     michaelclancy.com/

14. The Monroe Carell Jr. Children's Hospital at Vanderbilt
     University Medical Centre is now known around the world
     for pioneering prenatal spina bifida surgery:https://www.
     childrenshospitalvanderbilt.org/program/spina-bifida-clinic

15. Clancy asserted that, for legal purposes, it must be stated
     that this 'Story Behind the Picture' is his opinion of the
     events as they took place during the surgery for Samuel.

5
Children and Grief

O how shall summer's honey breath hold out
Against the wrackful siege of battering days
- Shakespeare, Sonnet 65

The play *Kids' Stuff* by Ramond Cousse opens with an eight-year old boy who has just been to a funeral:

> And I lay down on the bench with my grey coat so as
> not to catch cold and I said to myself let us try
> Let us try to be dead
> Let us try I lay down on the bench and I said to
> myself it is so I am dead
> I am dead as I had seen it in books on television in
> the newspapers everywhere at war in the movies at the
> cinema...[1]

From this compelling opening we are plunged into the young boy's review of his eight years of life as he seeks to understand the death of his best friend, Marcel. His rich and vivid memories of their friendship, including spying on Marcel's sister as she has sex with the local butcher's apprentice and the impassioned speeches of their frenzied schoolmaster, captured the innocence, the wonderment, and the sumptuous imagination of childhood. Finally, the young boy's reminiscences bring him back to the funeral:

> The priest arrives everyone gets up but the priest says
> You can be seated my brethren

He lifts his arms to the sky he sings he drinks from a big
glass
You must not weep my brethren
He says that if everyone weeps it is because everyone
believes that Marcel is dead
But rejoice my brethren I am going to announce the
good news
Marcel is not dead he is in eternal life
I rejoice Marcel was not dead anymore the priest said it
in his church…

The funeral procession weaves its way to the cemetery.
Marcel's coffin is lowered into the grave and people throw
water onto it but witnessing this ceremony does nothing
for the young boy's grasp of the situation:

I went back the next day to the edge of the hole to help
Marcel come out but there was not any more hole just
some fresh dirt and white flowers
I was happy I said to myself Marcel got out all alone
I run to his father's house I go up to his room but
Marcel's father says to me
Where are you going my child
I am going to get Marcel
My child you know well enough that Marcel is no long-
er with us that he is dead forever
I say no Marcel is alive the priest said so in his church

This is the boy's first real encounter with death. Although
he has seen hearses pass by his house and observed that
only some of the people walking behind the hearses weep
and whilst he has witnessed the butcher slaughter sheep
and cattle and young calves and felt sadness at their demise,
loss has not really impacted on his young world. Marcel is

his best friend and Marcel is the one with whom he fights and plays corks. Now Marcel has gone and he is full of questions: What is dead? Where is Paradise? Looking for understanding, the words of the priest and Marcel's father only confuse and frighten him. In trying to come to grips with these new feelings of desolation and despair, the small boy has been cast aside by the religious adult world. All he can do is live with the bewildering torment:

> I did not know if Marcel was dead if Marcel was alive
> I did not see him anymore ever in the street I did not
> see him anymore ever in his room anymore ever at the
> cemetery
> I did not see him anymore ever anywhere
> I did not see Marcel anymore ever anywhere I only saw
> him in my head at night when he told me to go wait for
> him in his room.

So he visits Marcel in his dreams, but in his dreams the young boy is placed into a coffin and carried through the streets in a hearse. His family and community follow in a line and he is lowered into an empty grave. At first he is joyous with the anticipation of seeing Marcel again 'at the bottom of the hole.' Instead he finds himself alone, abandoned alive in the grave in the darkness with dirt thundering onto the top of the wooden coffin and only distant dying laughter to comfort him.

This work explores how a young child is denied the opportunity to learn how to manage his pain and anxiety when he loses his closest friend because no one around him really knows how to deal with their own deep and immense sorrow. Instead what he learns about grief from this encounter is to not talk about death, to bottle up his feelings, and to isolate himself. Here is grief at its formation, beginning its inevitable pathway. For unless informed otherwise, he will approach loss and grief in the same way as he has been taught to do with the death of Marcel.

Kids' Stuff was based on Cousse's own early experiences and adapted from his novel *Enfantillages*. Cousse was born on 20 April 1942 at Saint-Germain en Laye in France. In programme notes for the 1998 season of the play performed at the Ensemble Theatre, Sydney, Australia, translator Katharine Sturak wrote of Cousse: 'Built like a mini-tank, a compulsive talker and hearty eater, he had just returned from the Avignon Festival in the south of France where he had had great success performing the boy in *Kids' Stuff*. I was instantly entranced by the profound simplicity of the character, and the universal experience of childhood that he had captured in this largely autobiographical work. The perfection of his text needed no interpretation, no adaptation. It simply is, like a prayer, like a mantra, and translating it was effortless.' Cousse wrote three successful dramatic monologues, which he performed himself, yet he took his own life on 22 December 1991 at the age of forty-nine.[2] Such a decisive gesture suggests that, more than a creative exploration of a young boy's first encounter with death, the play was instead Cousse's cry for help for his own unresolved grief.

How can a parent help their child deal with grief?

Grief is a confused jumble of complicated and painful memories. Children, like adults, will have things they wished they had said to the person who has died, things they regretted saying, and the desire to continue to experience the future with the person who has died. With the chance to say or correct these things gone, the emptiness that is left has emotional value for the child and needs to be given voice. If that is stopped by adult intellect, these unexpressed emotions will continue to revolve as unconscious loops inside the child's head, stockpiled just below the conscious Plimsoll line and requiring energy to prevent them from escaping. The truth is that children will respond fully to grief experiences until they are taught to do otherwise. They will express a range of emotions, evaluate and conclude what is unfinished for them, and then move on. They also imprint adult reactions with alarming speed and begin to shut down on this ability to grieve fully anywhere from ages three to seven.[3] We help our children to express grief by:

1. Understanding how our children unconsciously absorb our emotional patterns and replicate them.

2. Recognising the emotional connection our child had to the person who has died.

3. Our being aware of the circumstances of the death and the impact this might have on our child, not just us.

4. Truthfully expressing how you, as a parent, are feeling.

Emotional replication

We are a map of our parents, learning from them how to react emotionally and how to be in the world. One has only to observe small children and their parents together to see the patterns of mimicry that are unconsciously at work. Our parents teach us what they have been taught which is what our grandparents taught them and our great-grandparents taught our grandparents. This way of passing on information travels forwards through the generations. Our emotional history contributes just as much to our personal identity as our genetic makeup contributes to our physical stature. So it is with grief. Initially we learn how to grieve from our parents, but if they have been taught incomplete ways of expressing and dealing with loss, they will pass on emotional replication. By refusing to talk about death with the young boy in *Kids' Stuff*, his family and his community were teaching him to repress his feelings. When children are discouraged from expressing strong emotions, their sense of isolation increases, for they are acutely aware of an undercurrent of disapproval and condemnation and sensitive to the fact that their actions are being judged and criticised. In a short time they learn superficial behaviour patterns that no longer expose their vulnerability. What the young boy knew about death came from an illusion:

> I am dead as I had seen it in books on television in
> the newspapers everywhere at war in the movies at the
> cinema...'

His community, the priest, continued that illusion:

> Marcel is not dead he is in eternal life

And, finally, not even his mother could help him:

> I ask my mother loudly what does it mean eternal life
> but my mother says softly One must not talk at funerals

The young boy grasps from his mother's reaction that, even at the funeral, the place where it would have been at its most appropriate to talk about the death of his best friend, he must not do so. We assume adults know what they are doing. This is often a false assumption. Society has developed the following injunctions to keep us from talking about our feelings of intense loss:

> 'Be strong. Your children need you.'
> 'If you're going to cry, go to your room.'
> 'Keep busy. You'll deal with it better.'
> 'What's done is done. You have to move on.'
> 'Put on a brave face to the world.'

These statements do nothing to help us resolve the accumulation of emotions that arise as a result of the loss. The unspoken message is: 'Don't show your feelings', yet grief is, by definition, the emotional response to loss. Annie, a woman now in her early sixties, remembered an event from her past which illustrates this restrictive belief:

> In 1978, when I was twenty-three years old, my father committed suicide after my mother left him. We, as a family, drew together and didn't receive counselling. I couldn't talk about my father's death for many years. Even now I am greatly saddened by the whole event. My brother, who was the one who found him, was the most affected. I still can't watch movies where people shoot themselves.
>
> My husband advised me not to discuss this with anyone, so I didn't. It was only years later that I told my best friend what really happened.

For my own part, for as long as I can remember my parents were part of the *Chevra Kadisha*, a voluntary organisation of men and women within the Jewish community whose sole function was the care of the dead from the time of death until burial. This guardianship, known as *Chesed*

Shel Emes, represents an act of genuine kindness, since it can never be repaid by the recipient. Women attending women and men attending men would undertake *Tahara*, the preparation of the body in accordance with Jewish tradition through ritual purification and the dressing of it in traditional shrouds. Since death did not have a timetable, my parents could be called out at a moment's notice. This care of the dead, this act of kindness, was part of what my parents did, yet somehow it was different when it came to grief. When I was twelve, my ninety-one-year-old grandfather died at home in the early hours of the morning. My mother was in hospital and so it was his son, my father, who woke me up. 'Grandpa's dead,' he told me. 'Do you want to see his body?' I hesitated. The house we lived in was the one he'd built. I had lived with him all my life. I heard my voice as from a distance, cracked and strained, 'I don't …know….' A man of few words, my father squeezed my hand. 'You don't have to,' he whispered and then he was gone. I dressed and made my way downstairs to my grandfather's room, then froze in the doorway. The bed was made, the white coverlet drawn over a bed neatened too soon for the time of day. My stomach knotted. My grandfather was gone and I hadn't said goodbye. Too late I realised my father had heard me say 'know' and translated that as 'no'. My father was a gentle man and felt the loss deeply, but there were other burdens on him at the time. It wasn't until twenty-three years later as a published playwright that I finally realised how unresolved was that childhood grief and how it had remained an unconscious time warp of sorrow, permeating my life with its own colour of guilt and remorse. I did not know then what

I know now, that I had to make grief my friend in the turmoil of life.

The emotional connection of your child to the person who has died

The relationships we have with one another across our lifetime are unique and the emotional responses we have when they die will be in proportion to that relationship's depth and value. If your child's attachment to their grandparent or aunt or uncle was strong and a deep bond has been forged, then their death will produce a powerhouse of emotional energy. If your child had little contact with that relative, then their death may produce few emotions. As well, not all children love the relatives that you, as their parents, love. It may also be the case that you had a difficult or awkward relationship with a relative whom your child loves. By maintaining a neutral stance in the situation, you allow your child to discover what is unprocessed or fragmentary in that relationship without adult agendas confusing the issue. The emotional bonds children make and their need for relationship and intimacy are crucial for their emotional security and in contributing to their happiness and wellbeing. The successful conclusion to these bonds and attachments is just as significant.

The circumstances of the death

Death comes as a shock at the best of times. That loss will be compounded if the death is sudden or unexpected, or if there is mutilation or disfigurement such as from a car accident, a murder, a suicide or a long, drawn-out illness. In this extreme situation, without opportunity to prepare for the loss or say goodbye, the child not only has to process the separation from parent or relative, but also the complete visual transformation of someone they loved. The trauma can stimulate intense reactions such as shock, anger, guilt, sudden depression, despair, and hopelessness, as well as Post Traumatic Stress Disorder, all of which may take years to reconcile and cause the child to step away from life as a survival mechanism. The pitch of the family also changes. Along with the devastation of the primary loss there may also be unforeseen secondary losses: loss of income, loss of home, loss of social status or parental marital problems, all of which will affect the child. If the child was also involved in the disaster or was physically injured, further difficulties occur, resulting in survivor guilt, feelings of numbness, unreality and fear and a closed loop of virulent memories.[4]

The ability of the parent to express truthfully what they are feeling

Children need others to mirror as they grow and will follow role models on a consistent basis without question. In the feature film *The American President*, the character of Lewis Rothschild, the American President's Chief Domestic Policy Advisor, put it this way:

> People want leadership. And in the absence of genuine
> leadership, they will listen to anyone who steps up to
> the microphone. They want leadership, Mr. President.
> They're so thirsty for it, they'll crawl through the
> desert toward a mirage, and when they discover there's
> no water, they'll drink the sand.[5]

While Lewis was referring to adults, children are no different. If you shut down on expressing emotion, your child will copy this. Furthermore, if you are so deeply grieving, or in shock from the death of a loved one, you may not be capable of communicating clearly with your child, however much you may want to do so. In these circumstances there is another option. Margaret C. recounted this to me:

> In 1993 I lost my mum to cancer just ten days after the birth of my second son. I remember being at my dad's house several days after Mum had died — my siblings and their families were there — and my older son Benjamin, who was two at the time and struggling with what we later discovered was dyspraxia, was riding his little fire engine round and round in circles in the lounge. Suddenly he stopped, and in that classic moment of absolute silence that sometimes happens when a load of people stop talking all at once, he asked, 'Where's Grandma?' With Matthew about two weeks old at that time, I was still grappling with the massive hormonal overload from the birth, alongside massive shock from the death of my beloved mum, so I hadn't even really thought about how to talk to him about what had happened. My sister-in-law immediately chirped up nice and loudly, 'She's gone to sleep darling', before I could organise my thoughts enough to respond. I might not have had the answer myself at that point, but I knew that definitely wasn't it. I spoke to my GP, the health visitor, and the midwife, but all of their suggestions involved me trying to talk to Benjamin as if he was older, or read stories he wouldn't really understand, and besides which I was so upset to the point of being nearly incoherent with tears — probably due to emotional overload —

that if I tried to talk about it to him, I knew I would break down, and I didn't want him to see me that upset.

It was our cranial osteopath who came up with the idea to talk to him when he was asleep, so that if I dissolved into tears and was unable to continue, it wouldn't matter. So I waited until he was deeply asleep and sat by his bed, waiting for the words to come. They did, along with many, many tears, but it was profoundly healing because I could say a whole load of stuff that he probably wouldn't have understood if he'd been awake — and in fact I was strangely a lot calmer than if I'd tried to do it when he *was* awake. I know that I got through to him on a completely different level, because he seemed to be much more at peace in the following days and when I asked him about it recently he says he doesn't really have much memory of that time — which I think must be a good thing. Both boys have seen me upset about losing my parents, and others we've lost along the way, so I know they (hopefully) have a good model to follow. I guess the point I want to make is that if there are times as a parent when the conflict between being deeply grieving yet having to be there for your child becomes too great, talking to them in their sleep definitely works.

When it comes to grief, the most precious gift you, as a parent can give your child is to tell the truth about how you are feeling without assigning blame to any external mechanism or judging your feelings, no matter how difficult they are to express. Children think literally and need concrete terms in order to be clear about the situation. Answering their questions simply and honestly and using the word 'death', rather than euphemisms like 'passed away', sets a clear framework for them. They don't need great detail and if you have shown willingness to engage with them about the situation and your feelings, they will ask if they want to know more. Their body language will tell you whether they are listening because this is a new situation with which they are trying to grapple (focused, attentive, eye contact) or whether they are staying there for your benefit (agitated, fidgety, little or no eye contact). In this way a child learns that it is safe to reveal any and all of their feelings about their relationship with the one who has died without the confusion of adult approval. This allows them to build their self-confidence in expressing emotional truth in the face of future losses, both large and small.

Managing emotions

Managing emotions and educating a child on how to do this begins early. Continually feeding children statements of value ('you are bad') wedded to statements of blame ('you make me angry') means they constantly learn to hand over responsibility for how they feel to other people and become endlessly manipulated by other people's needs. Statements that place the person in the centre of their emotional world (statements that begin with 'I feel…') allow the person to take responsibility for their feelings and to manage their emotions. When you tell your child, 'I feel angry at your behaviour' and discuss that behaviour with them ('This is what happened when you took this action and next time I would like you to think more carefully before you do that') your child learns that it is their behaviour that is under discussion and not their inherent right to be loved. It also allows your child to modify their behaviour next time and empowers them to access their own internal states ('How am I feeling?') rather than having feelings assigned to them by others who may not have their best interests at heart or who may not understand their situation ('They are angry' = 'It is my fault' = 'I am powerless to feel other than angry'). This has immediate benefits when connected with grief. When your child feels safe enough to tell you, 'I feel angry that my brother died', this means you can guide your child to explore this feeling more fully. It may take days, weeks, months and years for all the other emotions connected with this statement to be fully fleshed out, but now their feelings have a pathway for completion, it is no longer a closed system.

Staying alert to how we, as adults, send these messages to our children takes focus. A good example of this is the experience of Ruth, who was saying goodbye to her sister who was moving to another country. It was clearly an emotional time for her, and her two small children, sensing her distress without understating why, expressed this by demanding her attention. When Trent, her four-and-a-half year old, inadvertently bumped her and the plate she was holding dropped and broke, Ruth's reaction was to sit heavily in a chair, sigh vigorously and put her head into her hands, indicating she was holding back her temper. Trent immediately broke into tears for fear he was going to be blamed and punished. Dorothy, his younger sister, aged two-and-a-half years, immediately pointed at the broken plate and said to Trent in clear mimicry of her mother in anger, 'Look at what you've done!' In recalling this story, Ruth came to recognise that under stress she had reverted to patterns that her mother had used, that of blaming external causes for her emotions. If she had defused the situation by telling Trent that she loved him, that she was angry at his behaviour and that this room was not the place in which to run around and let off steam and asked him if he could suggest a better place to do that, she would have empowered him, teaching him about the appropriateness of space and how to handle his emotions. Indeed, if she had explained to both Trent and Dorothy before the arrival of her sister that this was probably the last time she would see their aunt for a long while and that she was feeling deeply saddened by this, she would have given them a clear template for expressing sorrow at loss.

In her work with an emotionally disturbed five-year old boy called Dibs, Virginia Axline, the originator of play therapy, recognised that Dibs could only grow in confidence if confidence was shown in him and that this could only be achieved in a two-fold process: first, by her understanding that every action he undertook had a reason behind it; second, in her having no hidden agendas in her actions towards him. This meant that she did not expect him to read her mind and come up with answers which met her unstated standards. This then gave Dibs the opportunity to see and feel the effects of his own reactions and in so doing, make them clear for himself, become conscious of them, and finally accept them.[6]

Loss as path-finders in adolescence

Where any two worlds meet, the point is sacred, the boundary often marked by stone or ritual. In the secular world these two worlds come together most clearly when we encounter death. We need boundaries between these worlds in order to avoid contamination.

Sean Kane suggested that there is an unseen balance between the Otherworld, the world of the enigmatic, and the mundane world where life takes shape and form.[7] The guardians of the threshold demand our attention and if it is difficult enough to pay those dues as an adult, how much more difficult is it to do so when a child and still being shaped in the ways of the world. In its best expression, however, these early losses can become the catalyst for that person's contribution to society. In the documentary film *Me and Isaac Newton*, two scientists came to an epiphany through such losses.[8] Dr Karol Sikora, Professor of Cancer Medicine at Hammersmith Hospital, London and (then) Chief of the World Health Organisation Cancer Program, was encouraged by his father, an electrical engineer, to read science books at the age of eight or nine. His father was a Polish migrant and ambitious for his son and he insisted that Sikora go to Oxford or Cambridge, after which he could do as he pleased. Sikora secured a place at Cambridge at the age of sixteen. 'He was a great friend,' said Sikora. Not long afterwards his father died from lung cancer. Sikora felt relieved that his father knew he had made it into Cambridge, but expressed the deep regret in the documentary film, made in 1999, that since his father would never see him grow to adulthood, they would never be able to have a beer in a pub together and enjoy the adult conversation that he now had with his own son. Even though at that time cancer was not seen to be one of the dominating illnesses of the twenty-first century, from his first year at medical school Sikora knew that he wanted to be a cancer specialist. 'I don't think (my father's death) influenced me going into cancer specifically,' he said, 'but it influenced me about medicine and communication with patients because communication in the 1960s was really poor with families, with patients, and so on.'

Dr Gertrude B. Elion (1918-1999), Pharmaceutical Chemist for Glaxo-Wellcome and 1988 Nobel Prize Winner, became interested in science at the age of fifteen, an age she considered fairly late in a young person's life. As she was getting ready to enter college, her grandfather, to whom she'd been extremely close as a child, died 'pretty horribly'. As she watched him die, she had the sudden realisation that what she wanted to do with her life was to become a chemist and find a cure for cancer. Once set upon this course, she never wavered from it. Later, engaged to be married to a man who developed a bacterial endocarditis and who died two years before the advent of penicillin, she recognised her pathway in life had been wholly determined by family loss. 'Everything seemed to say to me, if you do research and you discover cures for diseases, this is what your life is about.' Not every young person has profound career-invoking experiences such as these, yet all encounters with the boundary guardians are there to feed and nourish us, if we let them.

Edward - A Child In Grief

Julie was married to Daniel, an Anglican priest. Both were born and educated in Australia and moved to England when Daniel was offered work there. Edward was born 28 February 1985 and Julie described Daniel as 'an absolutely excellent father' in the first three years of Edward's life and in the next nineteen months as 'an extremely good father'. In

September 1989, when Edward was four-and-a-half years old, developing his resourcefulness and learning to reason, yet still only able to deal with one thing at a time, Daniel acknowledged that he was gay and left both of them. More than his confession, what shocked Julie was Daniel's lack of contact with Edward. Missing arranged meetings without explanation, Daniel simply disappeared from Edward's life. Although mobile phones were first invented in 1985, in 1989 they were nowhere near as prolific as today and there was certainly no such thing as text messaging to maintain contact. It was also to be another ten years before the drama series *Queer As Folk,* a drama serial set in Manchester's gay village, which chronicled the lives of Stuart, his best friend, Vince, and fifteen-year old Nathan who was in love with Stuart, appeared on television giving an establishment voice to the gay scene.[9] Indeed at that time all the gay discos in Brighton were in basements, so Daniel literally went underground. It was a vastly different story for Julie who just felt devastated.

Edward's first experience of loss and grief took them all to the sharp end of difficulty. His bodily response took over as a protective mechanism and whenever he became emotionally upset, he lost his vision. For their own survival Julie moved them both into a shared house with a family who, with love, understanding and homoeopathic medicine, helped nurture them through the next three months. While this period of time was a busy, happy time for Edward who, according to Julie, loved living with people and the stimulation that this brought, it was nevertheless a time of deep grief. As far as they were both concerned, without any contact whatsoever from Daniel, they had both been plunged into sudden loss. Proteus had come to call with a form of grief that is possibly the most punishing — the lament for a loved one who is still alive but not around physically, for without a body to view to make the event concrete and final, there is always hope that the person will return.

Julie, however, had to make a rapid decision. She had been advised by a lawyer that, unless she took immediate action, under the Hague Convention, once Daniel resurfaced there was a chance he could force her to stay in England at his whim. In mid-January 1990 Julie and Edward returned to Sydney, Australia. Edward was due to start school and the Australian school year began in February. It was a turning point for both of them. With no financial or emotional support from Daniel, Julie found work and endeavoured to hold things together. Later she reflected: 'I thought that I was doing the right thing bringing him back to a supportive family and in some ways it was the right thing — but it was too much too soon.' A change of residence for a child is a loss of basic bricks-and-mortar security. A change of country is a loss of environment, culture and friendships. Connected with the loss of his father, the number of external changes that were occurring in such a short period of time for Edward was disproportionate. The return to Australia proved to be the moment of impact. The key to living in England was to dress in layers (vests, shirts with buttons, coats with buttons, scarf and gloves), all of which required dexterity, a task Edward managed easily. In Australia he was unable to perform even the simple action of pulling on a T-shirt and shorts. Engulfed with unexplained emotional pain at the loss of father, house, home, and friends, Edward's way of coping was to throw massive tantrums, the primal cry for help from someone drowning in their own confusion, frustration and sorrow.

In mid-1990 Julie moved into a shared house with another mother and a young boy the same age as Edward. It was a happy household and Julie felt that life was secure enough for her to begin studying counselling. In class she met Alexander, another student, and they fell in love. Slowly that year they got to know each other. Julie would visit Alexander after Edward was asleep and on the one or two occasions that she spent the night with him, she made sure she was home by 6.30 am. Mostly Alexander stayed at their house and slowly Edward got to know his new step-father. Julie thought she was being a responsible parent and Alexander a thoughtful partner. Edward's perspective, however, was quite different, as she found out some years later.

In 1991 the unexpected happened. Daniel returned to Australia and once more became part of their lives. Edward began seeing his father every fortnight when, as Julie put it, Daniel would do all the 'fun' stuff with him, but without any real sense of responsibility. Nevertheless life settled into such a regular pattern that in 1992 Julie and Alexander moved in together. In February 1994 an event occurred that puzzled Julie. Daniel remembered Edward's ninth birthday, yet Julie knew it was not like Daniel to be so thoughtful. Julie paid him a visit, sharing her curiosity at the birthday card and sensing a difficulty he was not voicing. Daniel went white. He suggested she pour herself a glass of wine and sit down. Then he told her that he had AIDS and that he had known this for about a year. Julie felt her stomach fall away. Apart from her own feelings, she was faced with a dilemma: should she tell Edward or not? Tossing the problem around in her mind she finally decided that telling him was the best possible solution.

Once Julie knew of Daniel's diagnosis, she and Alexander could plan how best to deal with the situation. In April 1994, Julie told him that his Daddy was extremely ill. Edward asked if he was going to die and Julie said, yes, eventually, and it was going to be difficult. Julie, Edward, and Alexander discussed the situation extensively. They made a list of the people they wanted to tell, double-checking that Edward felt secure discussing it with them. This also included his grandmother. Julie's family and some of her friends were furious with her for telling Edward, saying he was too young to cope with death. Julie thought otherwise.

In the intervening months left to them, Edward saw a great deal of his father. It was an extraordinarily close time and they told each other often how much they loved each other. Daniel wore an amethyst pendant and he made it clear to Edward that after he died, Edward could keep it as a communication memento between them. In August 1995 Daniel made the decision to go to Melbourne in order to be near a priest who was like a father to him. He booked himself into a hospice and kept in constant contact with Edward by phone. Five hours before his death he said a final, tearful good-bye to Edward. The date was 6 November 1995. Edward was nearly eleven years old and he had just reached out to Proteus.

Edward asked if he could see his father's body, so Julie booked train tickets for them both and together they travelled from Sydney to Melbourne. Julie had seen a dead body before and described it 'like seeing a waxworks body.'

AIDS, however, is an extremely cruel disease. Not only was she shocked at the deterioration in Daniel, but she could see that Edward was stunned and overwhelmed. Yet by viewing his father's body, Edward was confronting the fact that death was a permanent, irreversible, biological process. The priest who had been with Daniel when he died said to Edward: 'I know it's a shock to see your Daddy like this, but don't get caught up in the adult world. It's just a body and your daddy is with the angels. Let yourself feel what you're feeling and then talk about it because talking is a way of dealing with it and it will help.' So over the next two years (1996 and 1997) Julie, Edward and Alexander agreed that whenever Edward wanted to talk about his feelings, his father, his death and all that had happened, he could and they would listen.

In early 1996, with both of them in the embrace of grief, Julie was aware that Edward began to feel the hopelessness of loss and how it seemed to erode all that was important. There were two expressions of this in Edward's life. First, he began having a difficult time at school. Julie went to see the teacher and explained that Edward's father had just died. She was dismayed when the teacher replied: 'I don't care whose father's died, I treat all children equally.' Julie had no more joy with the headmaster, so they decided to change schools. This proved to be a wise decision. It was, however, a hard and difficult year for Edward. The second expression was that, to the absolute rage of all concerned, they found out that Edward's grandmother had taken the amethyst pendant from Daniel's body. With an aversion to squabbling, Julie remained detached from the process. Others, however, fought successfully on Edward's behalf and retrieved the amethyst. A great deal of emotional trauma was expended in the process. Edward considered the stone to have spiritual or metaphysical properties and to this day he keeps the amethyst next to his bedside and wears it from time to time.

In 1997, now twelve years old, Edward was in the centre of his grief and his life continued to be confused and disorganised. This was a year where, Julie said, Edward felt that authority figures had let him down in some way. Edward desperately wanted Julie and Alexander to get married, but this was not in Alexander's plans, so Edward showed Alexander the brunt of his temper. From mid-1997 to early 1998, Julie describes Edward as 'a particularly angry child', yet anger as an expression of untangling grief will often be projected onto a safe member of the household who can carry it for the person until it can be understood. This was Edward being tossed by the changes embodied by Proteus.

In 1998, the third year after his father's death, Edward's desire to constantly talk about his father began to naturally peter out. Edward became a little more romantic about Daniel, remembering only the good times and Julie had to work hard at grounding this romanticism with the reality she knew to be Edward's father. In this year Edward started senior school. Julie deliberately chose a Catholic humanistic school that embraced a stricter, more authoritarian framework than the more relaxed State/ public school system of his primary education. She also took into consideration that his father had been a priest and hoped the religious nature of the school would be beneficial to Edward's memory of him. Edward also started to become aware of girls.

In 1999, as he turned fourteen, the fourth year after his father's death, Julie said that everything unresolved re-surfaced and many hidden emotions were revealed. It was in this year that Edward confessed to Julie that during the first year of her relationship with Alexander, when he had woken in the night and needed her warmth and found her bed empty, he had felt abandoned. The depth of his feeling surprised her. It was so different from her experience of events that she found it hard to believe and yet she acknowledged that this was how he had experienced it and she felt upset about her past actions: 'I was the only continuum in his little life — the only person who had been there from babyhood to ages five-six.'

The intervening years saw Edward encounter the natural processes of adolescence. In May 2003, Julie wrote to me:

> Now that Edward is eighteen, he is treated pretty
> much like an adult in this house. I was greatly
> impressed with his school last year because their
> graduation ceremony was a real ritual into adulthood.
> It was such an appropriate time to use as a launch
> into me playing a different role in his life, that is, him
> having more freedom and independence. I also used
> it as an opportunity to hand over the responsibility
> of maintaining connections with his father's family.
> I have been doing this on his behalf since his father
> died. (Of course I will still have some connections).
> I encouraged him to make contact with his father's
> family in his own right. So he spent Christmas with
> them! Extremely different for me and totally healing
> for him. Although he got into Wine Marketing at

a traditional style university, he chose a Technical College course which is in line with his passion - sports! He is doing really well, studying for a Certificate in Sports (Coaching and Development). He has been having lots of fun exploring his new-found freedom, although I am starting to step in a little again by emphasising the need for him to start earning his own way in this household. One of his favourite songs is *Cat's in the Cradle*:

> And the cat's in the cradle and the silver spoon
> Little boy blue and the man in the moon
> When you coming home, dad?
> I don't know when
> But we'll get together then,
> You know we'll have a good time then.[10]

I must admit that this brings a few tears to my eyes.

Julie and Edward have stayed in touch with me over the years. In February 2019 Julie casually remarked to me what a lovely young man Edward had turned out to be. When I pressed her further, she added:

> Since 2003 Edward has grown from strength to strength, but not without some battles with his own emotional challenges. In 2005 Edward suffered from depression as he struggled to come to terms with the death of his father and growing up without a father. Since then he has overcome and learnt to manage his depression, married, and had two children of his own. He now works as a diversional therapist in the mental health arena in Melbourne, Australia. At 34 Edward is a wonderful young man who is adored by

his two children, his colleagues, and his clients. It is heart-warming to see this young man's contribution to society, his empathy with the downtrodden, his quirky sense of humour, and the positive attitude that he adopts in life.

When I asked Edward if he wanted to add a word of his own, he wrote:

> I have as an adult embraced those traumatic times and lessons as opportunities to learn and develop into a man. I enjoy the philosophy of Stoicism and am a consumer peer support worker at a psychiatric ward. So I'd like to add that from my grief I learnt the valuable lesson of valuing time, being engaged in the moment, and making the most of life!

Templates of completion

How a child reacts to the loss of their intimate kith and kin is influenced by many factors which include the child's age, their relationship to the person who has died, the strength and attachment of that relationship, the circumstances of the death, their perception and awareness of life and its process, and their understanding of death. It also depends on the willingness of those of us close to the child to talk freely and truthfully about our own emotions in order to help to create a safe place in which our child can express confusion and pain. The worst-case scenario will manifest as our child being blocked from expressing their feelings about the loss. The best-case scenario will allow them to take on new responsibilities in the light of the death. By telling Edward that his father had AIDS and was going to die, Julie consciously allowed him to engage with a shift of responsibility which in turn enabled his father and him to determine the shape of their remaining time together. Clearly the way Julie and Alexander guided Edward as he dealt with such intense loss at so young an age gave him a tremendous advantage in handling crises he had yet to encounter as an adult.

On top of all this, on a more personal level, the loss of a direct family member for our child is also a loss for us as their parent. Not only are we supporting our child's emotional landscape, but we are dealing with our own grief as well. Under such circumstances it is all too easy to unwittingly push our child aside. The more complete, yet extremely challenging path is to allow them to be part of the circle of loss. It takes courage to stay open to a child's grief.

Notes

1. Raymond Cousse, *Kids' Stuff*, trans. Katharine Sturak (Melbourne: Australian Nouveau Theatre Publications, 1984).
2. http://raymondcousse.chez.com/reperes.htm — accessed 2 May 2003.
3. John W. James, Russell Friedman, and Leslie Landon Matthews, *When Children Grieve: For Adults to Help Children Deal with Death, Divorce, Pet Loss, Moving, and Other Losses* (New York: HarperCollins, 2001), p.96.
4. P. Valent, 'Survivor Guilt,' in *Stress: Concepts and Cognition, Emotion, and Behavior*, ed. George Fink (London: Academic Press, 2016).pp.373-375.
5. Aaron Sorkin. *The American President*. © Castle Rock Entertainment and Universal City Studios, Inc. (1995) Screenplay at: http://www.dailyscript.com/scripts/american_president.html — accessed 24 November 2016.

6.   Virginia M. Axline, *Dibs: In Search of Self: Personality Development in Play Therapy* (Harmondsworth: Penguin Books, 1964).

7.   Sean Kane, *Wisdom of the Mythtellers* (Peterborough, Ontario: Broadview, 1994).

8.   Michael Apted (writer/director). *Me and Isaac Newton*. Producers: Jody Patton and Eileen Gregory. © Clear Blue Sky Productions Inc. Seattle, USA. (1999)

9.   Russell T. Davies (creator/writer/co-producer) *Queer As Folk* Producer: Nicola Shindler. © Red Production Company and Channel 4, London, UK. (1999)

10.   *Cat's In The Cradle* by Harry Chapin (lyrics by Sandra Chapin) was originally recorded on Chapin's album 'Verities & Balderdash', Elektra records, 1974.

6
Terminus

> In the midst of winter, I finally learned that there was in
> me an invincible summer.
> - Albert Camus, playwright/novelist (1913-1960)

A man walking down a road sees a ferocious lion. The lion
sees the man, emits a great roar and bounds towards him.
Fearful for his life, the man turns on his heels and flees. The
lion races after him, growling all the way, finally overtaking
the man who drops to the ground quivering and waits
to be eaten. The lion says to him: 'Why are you running
away? I have a message for you.'

The world of common day is crammed with messages about how we can learn to let go, but like the man
running from the lion, we fear they will destroy us. Minor losses and disappointments, expectations that never
come to fruition or different endings to situations force us
to reassess our situation and to replace these expectations
with other goals. Rather than listening to these messages and using them as ways to assess loss and develop ways
to release it, we tend to suppress them with food, medication, alcohol, drugs, material goods and fantasy. Everyone remembers and laughs at Otto, the character in *A Fish
Called Wanda* who opens a safe expecting to find twenty
million dollars' worth of jewellery and instead finds nothing.[1] We laugh at his reaction ('Disappointed!') because
there is a gulf of unspoken material between what he says
(a mild word) and how he says it (spoken in fury). Play-

wright Harold Pinter described this lacuna of speech as 'a necessary avoidance, a violent, sly, and anguished or mocking smoke screen which keeps the other in its place.'[2] It is this avoidance of what is really going on inside us and the fact that we are socialised to show a brave face to the world that causes emotional blockages that can have such devastating consequences when faced with major loss.

Grief is not a process that happens alone. It is a team effort, a dialogue with those we love, alive and dead. Later in *A Fish Called Wanda*, screenwriters Cleese and Crichton sum up what they see as the detrimental aspect of being English in a speech lawyer Archie Leach makes to American Wanda Gershwitz when they meet in a secret rendezvous:

> Wanda, do you have any idea what it's like being English? Being so correct all the time, being so stifled by this dread of doing the wrong thing, of saying to someone 'Are you married?' and hearing 'My wife left me this morning', or saying 'Do you have children?' and being told 'They all burned to death on Wednesday.' You see, Wanda, we're all terrified of embarrassment. That's why we're so... dead. Most of my friends are dead, you know. We have these piles of corpses to dinner.[3]

Cleese and Crichton were writing about a particular trait of the English in dealing with emotion, yet it also sums up most of modern western society's attitude to loss and grief: the fear of saying the wrong thing, the fear of not knowing how to respond to another's acute pain and discomfort. Pinter called this 'the weight of the unsaid and the unutterable'.

Author Diane Ackerman wrote, 'I don't want to get to the end of my life and find that I lived just the length of it. I want to have lived the width of it as well.' My friend, Pietro Ballinari, added, 'I want to have lived the height, the weight, the light, the dark, the colours, the circumference, the content, the complexity, the simplicity, the allness, the nothingness and much more of it as well.' To have lived well means we will experience loss and undergo grief, yet none of us are prepared for its impact on our lives. Instead we pretend that death does not exist and that grief will never touch us. Furthermore, since western society is unaccustomed to seeing the expression of grief in the community, preferring instead to placate it and hide it away, we are generally not aware of the intensity or duration of the pain involved unless we've experienced it ourselves.

Grief is marked by sacrifice — not the act of slaughtering or surrendering a possession in order to appease a god, nor the act of submission and becoming a martyr. The sacrifice of grief is the process of becoming sacred — *sacrum facere* — in the transitional space of the mandorla where the only obligation is to listen to what is going on inside us. Then and only then can we begin to harness the natural grief review that occurs inside us with the loss, and ultimately bring the unique and lacerating pain of grief to a conclusion in ways that heal us, rather than destroy us. This will not happen in just a few weeks. The process continues out of sequence and with surprise. There is, however, a narrative and a story that will reveal itself in time. As Sean Kane noted, 'a death with no story is no death at all. A death that cannot be told is an unfinished life.'[4]

Grief isn't an event. It is an ever-changing process that takes place over time. It is Lying Down with the Seals; it is encountering Proteus in order to deal with the slippage between reality as we have known it and what it has now become as a result of the loss of a loved one. Our best response — to ourselves and to anyone in grief — is to be present in this sacred space and to recognise the nature of what lies ahead. David Almond described the journey of Persephone, struggling through the darkness to bring spring to earth in his novel *Skellig*. It could as easily be applied to the journey of grief, and in so doing, it reminds us to maintain hope in the darkest of hours:

> We thought of Persephone for a while in silence. I imagined her struggling her way towards us. She squeezed through black tunnels. She took wrong turnings, banged her head against the rocks. Sometimes she gave up in despair and she just lay weeping in the pitch darkness. But she struggled on. She waded through icy underground streams. She fought through bedrock and clay and iron ore and coal, through fossils of ancient creatures, the skeletons of dinosaurs, the buried remains of ancient cities. She burrowed past the tangled roots of great trees. She was torn and bleeding but she kept telling herself to move onward and upward. She told herself that soon she'd see the light of the sun again and feel the warmth of the world again.[5]

Knowing the shape of grief and its consequences over time means we carry a light, however small, along this pitch-black pathway to give edges and boundaries to this most relevant of rituals. Such a light enables us ultimately to encounter our changed future with focus, determination, and understanding when grief comes to call.

Notes

1. John Cleese and Charles Crichton. *A Fish Called Wanda* (London: Methuen, 1988), p.15.
2. Harold Pinter. *Various Voices.* (London: Faber and Faber 1998), p.19.
3. Cleese and Crichton, p.58.
4. Sean Kane. *Wisdom of the Mythtellers.* (Peterborough, Ontario: Broadview 1994), p.208.
5. David Almond. *Skellig* (London: Hodder Children's Books 1998), p.138.

Bibliography

Allende, Isabel. *Paula*. Barcelona: Plaza & Jane (1994).

Almond, David. *Skellig*. London: Hodder Children's Books (1998).

Axline, Virginia M. *Dibs: In Search of Self: Personality Development in Play Therapy*. Harmondsworth: Penguin Books (1964).

Bee, Peta. "Love Drug: Why Women Are Getting into Anabolic Steroids." London: *The Independent On Sunday*, 2 March 2003.

Boss, Pauline. *Ambiguous Loss: Learning to Live with Unresolved Grief*. Cambridge, Massachusetts: Harvard University Press (1999).

Brady, Bernadette. "Cycles within Cycles." *Wellspring Astrology Guide* (2002).

Bryant, Clifton D., and Dennis L. Peck. *Encyclopedia of Death and the Human Experience*. Vol. 1, Los Angeles: SAGE (2009).

Butler, R. N. "Recall and Retrospection." *Journal of the American Geriatrics Society*, no. 11 (1963): 523-29.

———. "The Life Review: An Interpretation of Reminiscence in the Aged." *Psychiatry* 26 (1963): 65-70.

Campbell, Joseph. *The Hero with a Thousand Faces*. London: Paladin (1988).

Chittick, William C., and Jalāl al-Dīn Rūmī (Maulana). *The Sufi Path of Love: The Spiritual Teachings of Rumi*. Suny Series in Islamic Spirituality. Albany: State University of New York Press (1983).

Coleman, Peter G. "Ageing and Life History: The Meaning of Reminiscence in Late Life." *The Sociological Review* 37, no. S1 (1989): 120-43.

Cousse, Raymond. *Kids' Stuff*. Translated by Katharine Sturak. Melbourne: Australian Nouveau Theatre Publications (1984).

Croally, N. T., and Roy Hyde. *Classical Literature: An Introduction*. London: Routledge (2011).

Dickens, Charles. *Oliver Twist*. London: Chapman & Hall Ltd (1907).

Eliade, Mircea. *The Sacred and the Profane: The Nature of Religion*. Translated by Willard R. Trask. Orlando: Harcourt, Inc. (1957).

Elkins, James. *Pictures and Tears: A History of People Who Have Cried in Front of Paintings*. New York: Routledge (2001).

Frank, Marcos G., Naoum P. Issa, and Michael P. Stryker. "Sleep Enhances Plasticity in the Developing Visual Cortex." *Neuron* 30 (1970): 275-87.

Franks, David D. "The Neuroscience of Emotions." In *Handbook of the Sociology of Emotions*, edited by Jan E. Stets and Jonathan H. Turner, 38-62. New York: Springer (2006).

Frey II, William H., and Muriel Langseth. *Crying: The Mystery of Tears*. Minneapolis, MN: Winston Press (1985).

Friedman, Russell, and John W. James. "Legacy of Love or Monument to Misery" Grief Recovery (UK) Ltd, http://www.griefrecoverymethod.co.uk/legacy-of-love-or-monument-to-misery/.

Furth, Gregg M. *The Secret World of Drawings: A Jungian Approach to Healing through Art*. 2nd ed. Toronto: Inner City Books (2002).

Gais, Steffen and Jan Born. 'Declarative Memory Consolidation: Mechanisms Acting During Human Sleep.' *Learning & Memory 11*, no. 6 (2004): 679-685.

Greenblatt, Stephen, Walter Cohen, Jean E. Howard, and Katharine Eisaman Maus, eds. *The Norton Shakespeare*. New York: W.W. Norton & Company, Inc. (1997).

Haber, David. "Life Review: Implementation, Theory, Research, and Therapy." *International Journal of Aging and Human Development* 63, no. 2 (2006): 153-71.

Helsing, K. J., M. Szklo, and G.W. Comstock. "Factors Associated with Mortality after Widowhood." *American Journal of Public Health* 71, no. 8 (1981): 802-09.

Homer. *The Odyssey*. Translated by E. V. Rieu. Harmondsworth: Penguin Books (1946).

Hunt, Jan. *The Natural Child: Parenting from the Heart*. Gabriola Island: New Society Publishers (2001).

Iles, Susanne. "The Storied Garden: Planting the Seeds of Myth." *Spirituality & Health* 5 (June 2002): 44.

James, John W., and Russell Friedman. *The Grief Recovery Handbook*. New York: Harper Collins (1998).

James, John W., Russell Friedman and Leslie Landon Matthews. *When Children Grieve: For Adults to Help Children Deal with Death, Divorce, Pet Loss, Moving, and Other Losses*. New York: HarperCollins (2001).

Johnson, Robert A. *Owning Your Own Shadow: Understanding the Dark Side of the Psyche*. HarperSanFrancisco (1991).

Jones, Rhian. *Emerging Patterns of Literacy: A Multidisciplinary Perspective*. London: Routledge (1996).

Kane, Sean. *Wisdom of the Mythtellers*. Peterborough, Ontario: Broadview (1994).

Kottler, Jeffrey A. *The Language of Tears*. San Francisco: Jossey-Bass Publishers (1996).

Kübler-Ross, Elisabeth, and Mal Warshaw. *Working It Through*. New York: Macmillan (1982).

Lamm, Maurice. *The Jewish Way in Death and Mourning*. New York: Jonathan David Publications (1969).

Lerner, Harriet Goldhor. *The Dance of Anger: A Woman's Guide to Changing the Patterns of Intimate Relationships* (New York: Harper Collins, 1985).

Leunig, Michael. *The Prayer Tree*. Melbourne: CollinsDove (1991).

Levine, Stephen. *Who Dies? An Investigation of Conscious Living and Conscious Dying*. New York: Anchor Press (1982).

Lewis, C. S. *A Grief Observed*. New York: Bantam Books (1963).

Lewis, Donald W., Margaret T. Middlebrook, Lissa Mehallick, Trudy Manning Rauch, Carole Deline, and Elise F. Thomas. 'Pediatric Headaches: What Do the Children Want?' *Headache: The Journal of Head and Face Pain* 36 (1996): 224-230.

Liston, Conor, and Jerome Kagan. 'Brain Development: Memory Enhancement in Early Childhood.' *Nature* 419, no. 6910 (2002): 896.

Maddison, David, and Wendy L. Walker. "Factors Affecting the Outcome of Conjugal Bereavement." *The British Journal of Psychiatry* 113, no. 503 (1967): 1057-67.

Marris, Peter. "Grief, Loss of Meaning and Society." *Bereavement Care* 11, no. 2 (1992/06/01 1992): 18-22.

———. *Loss and Change*. London: Routledge & Kegan Paul (1974) [1986].

———. *The Politics of Uncertainty: Attachment in Private and Public Life*. London: Routledge (1996).

Maudsley, Henry. *The Pathology of Mind: A Study of Its Distempers Deformities and Disorders*. London: Macmillan & Co (1895).

McKissock, Mal. "Bereavement and Grief." Interview by Norman Swan. *Health Report* (2001).

———. *Coping with Grief*, 4th ed. (Sydney: ABC Enterprises, 1985).

Mednick, Sara, Ken Nakayama, and Robert Stickgold. "Sleep-Dependent Learning: A Nap Is as Good as a Night." *Nature Neuroscience* 6, no. 7(07/print 2003): 697-98.

Orona, Celia J. "Temporality and Identity Loss Due to Alzheimer's Disease." In *Grounded Theory in Practice*, edited by Anselm L. Strauss and Juliet M. Corbin. Thousand Oaks, CA: Sage Publications (1997).

Oschman, James L., and Nora H. Oschman. "Somatic Recall Part 1 - Soft Tissue Memory." *Massage Therapy Journal* 34, no. 3 (1995).

Pinter, Harold. *Various Voices*. (London: Faber and Faber 1998).

Piontelli, Alessandra. From *Fetus to Child: An Observational and Psychoanalytic Study* (London: Routledge, 1992).

Proust, Marcel. *Swann's Way*. Translated by C.K.Scott Moncreiff. À La Recherche Du Temps Perdu, 1913-1927 (In Search of Lost Time). Edited by William C. Carter Vol. 1, (New Haven and London: Yale University Press, 2013).

Schwab, Reiko. 'A Child's Death and Divorce: Dispelling the Myth', *Death Studies* 5 (1998).

Sirota, Anton, Jozsef Csicsvari, Derek Buhl, and György Buzsáki. "Communication between Neocortex and Hippocampus During Sleep in Rodents." *Proceedings of the National Academy of Sciences of the United States of America* 100, no. 4 (2003): 2065–69.

Spretnak, Charlene. *The Resurgence of the Real: Body, Nature, and Place in a Hypermodern World*. New York; London: Routledge (1999).

Sweet, Jeffrey. *The Dramatist's Toolkit: The Craft of the Working Playwright*. Portsmouth, N.H.: Heinemann (1993).

Trismegistus, Hermes. *Liber Hermetis*. Translated by Robert Zoller. Edited by Robert Hand Salisbury, Queensland: Spica Publications (1998).

Twain, Mark, and John S. Tuckey. *Which Was the Dream?: The Mark Twain Papers and Other Symbolic Writings*. Berkeley and Los Angeles: University of California Press (1967).

Tynan, Kathleen. *The Life of Kenneth Tynan*. London: Weidenfeld and Nicolson (1987).

Valent, P. 'Survivor Guilt'. In *Stress: Concepts and Cognition, Emotion, and Behavior*, edited by George Fink, 373-376. London: Academic Press (2016).

Waldrop, M. Mitchell. *Complexity: The Emerging Science at the Edge of Order and Chaos.* New York: Simon & Schuster (1993).

Walker, Matthew, and J. Allan Hobson. "Neuroimaging and the Sleeping Brain." *Neuron* 28, no. 3 (2000): 629–33.

Walker, Peter. "Spiralling Anabolic Steroid Use Leaves UK Facing Health Timebomb, Experts Warn." *The Guardian,* 19 June 2015.

Wilcox, Ella Wheeler. *Poems of Passion.* Belford, Chicago: Clarke & Co. (1883).

Woodward, Joan. *The Lone Twin: A Study in Bereavement and Loss* (London: Free Association Books, 1998).

Worden, J. William. *Grief Counseling and Grief Therapy: A Handbook for the Mental Health Practitioner.* 2nd ed.: Springer Publishing Co. (1991).

Young, J. Z. *The Life of Mammals: Their Anatomy and Physiology.* Oxford: Clarendon Press (1957).

Index